READWELL'S

LEARN RUSSIAN
IN A MONTH

**Easy Method of Learning Russian
Through English Without a Teacher**

By :
Mrs. Rekha Chawla
B.A. (Cairo)

GW00514701

Readwell Publications
NEW DELHI-110008

Published by :
READWELL PUBLICATIONS
B-8, Rattan Jyoti, 18, Rajendra Place
New Delhi-110 008 (INDIA)
Phone : 25737448, 25712649, 25721761
Fax : 91-11-25812385
E-mail : readwell@sify.com
          newlight@vsnl.net

© All Rights including subject-matter, style are reserved
   with the Publisher.

ISBN 81-87782-18-8

Printed at : Arya Offset Press, New Delhi.

PREFACE

When I decided to learn Russian I was thinking that it would be an uphill task. As I progressed in the process of learning I found it easy and interesting. After learning Russian I felt that if it is properly taught learners would relish learning. By keeping all the problems which I had to face while learning I have tried to simplify the method of learning. I feel that if a person knows one language he can learn another easily.

The book is very scientifically planned particularly for the beginners who know a bit of English. I have, first of all, familiarised the readers with Russian Alphabet and this is necessary for a beginner. Then I have drawn parallels between English and Russian grammar restricting myself to only those aspects which are necessary for a learner. Expressions for conversation meant for different occasions and different places will give a fairly good working knowledge of the language. I don't claim that the book gives a thorugh knowledge of the language; it is the springboard which can help you dive deep into the subject to fish out pearls of the language.

I would thank the publishers for taking pains in bringing an error-free book.

Suggestions for improvement are welcome.

—Author

CONTENTS

ALPHABETS

In this section, the words are disposed in the order of the Russian Cyrillic alphabet. The order, with the names of the letters, is as follows:

А	а	ah		С	с	ehs
Б	б	beh		Т	т	teh
В	в	veh		У	у	oo
Г	г	geh		Ф	ф	ehf
Д	д	deh		Х	х	khah
Е	е	ё yeh (yaw)		Ц	ц	tseh
Ж	ж	zheh		Ч	ч	cheh
З	з	zeh		Ш	ш	shah
И	и	ee		Щ	щ	shchah
Й	й	ee KRAHT-kuh-yeh (lit., short i)		ъ		yehr (or TV'AWR-dy znahk)
К	к	kah		ы		yi-RY
Л	л	ehl		ь		yehr' or (M'AHKH-kee znahk)
М	м	ehm				
Н	н	ehn		Э	э	eh
О	о	aw		Ю	ю	yoo
П	п	peh		Я	я	yah
Р	р	ehr				

The letters ъ, ы, ь never occur in initial position in a Russian word, hence are not usually capitalized. They may appear in an inscription that is written completely in capitals, in which case they assume the same shape as the corresponding small letters, but in capital size.

RUSSIAN ALPHABET AND KEY TO PRONUNCIATION

Letter		Name of letter	Sound value	Corresponds to the English
Printed	Written			
А а	*Аа*	а	[а]	
Б б	*Бб*	бэ	[б]	b in **but**
В в	*Ввв*	вэ	[в]	v in **voice**
Г г	*Гг*	гэ	[г]	g in **get**
Д д	*Дд*	дэ	[д]	
Е е	*Ее*	е	[йэ]	ye in **yet**
Ё ё	*Ёё*	ё	[йо]	yo in **York**
Ж ж	*Жж*	жэ	[ж]	
З з	*Зз*	зэ	[з]	z in **zone**
И и	*Ии*	и	[и]	ee in **meet**
Й й	*Йй*	и крáткое	[й]	
К к	*Кк*	ка	[к]	
Л л	*Лл*	эл	[л]	
М м	*Мм*	эм	[м]	m in **my**
Н н	*Нн*	эн	[н]	
О о	*Ооо*	о	[о]	
П п	*Пп*	пэ	[п]	
Р р	*Рр*	эр	[р]	
С с	*Сс*	эс	[с]	s in **small**
Т т	*Тт*	тэ	[т]	
У у	*Уу*	у	[у]	u in **put**
Ф ф	*Фф*	эф	[ф]	f in **fine**
Х х	*Хх*	ха	[х]	
Ц ц	*Цц*	цэ	[ц]	
Ч ч	*Чч*	чэ	[ч]	
Ш ш	*Шш*	ша	[ш]	

Letter		Name of letter	Sound value	Corresponds to the English
Printed	Written			
Щ щ	*Щщ*	ща	[щ]	
Ъ ъ	*ъ ъ*	твёрдый знак		
Ы ы	*ы*	ы	[ы]	
Ь ь	*ь ь*	мягкий знак		
Э э	*Ээ*	э	[э]	e in ten
Ю ю	*Юю ю*	ю	[йу]	you in youth
Я я	*Яя*	я	[йа]	ya in yard

The older Russian alphabet, used under the Tsars, contained also: the letter i, interchangeable in value, but not in use, with и; i was used regularly in connection with another vowel (Россія, today spelled Россия); the letter ъ, which was silent, but served to indicate a "hard," or nonpalatal pronunciation of the preceding consonant; it appeared for the most part at the end of words, very seldom within the word; in the latter position, which is exceedingly rare, it has been retained, for the purpose of keeping unpalatalized a consonant which would otherwise be palatalized by a following palatal vowel; the letter ѣ, interchangeable in value, but not in use, with е; the letters v and θ, interchangeable in value, respectively, with и and ф, and used in religious words borrowed from the Greek (сvнод, synod; каѳедра, pulpit).

Vowel Sounds

a = father (stressed); bacon, (unstressed): карандаш, pencil;

e = yes (more or less distinct, according as it is stressed or unstressed): есть, to eat; еда, food;

ē = Yorick : мёд, honey; •

• ē is always stressed; the stress will therefore not be indicated on words containing ē; written Russian (save in children's books) does not generally use the double dot on ē, with the result that beginners are often left in doubt whether ё or е is indicated.

и = machine: имя, name;

й = May (this character is never used after a consonant). Май, May;

о = or (stressed); bacon (unstressed): хорошо, well;

у = food: ухо, ear;

ы = rhythm (this sound has no exact equivalent in English; it is best described as an attempt to pronounce *feed* with the front part of the mouth and *food* with the back of the tongue, at the same time): был, was;

э = met: этот, this;

ь has no value of its own, but serves to palatalize the preceding consonant: говорить, to speak;

ю = *you*: люблю, I love;

я = *yard*: ярмарка, village fair; язык, tongue.

It is to be noted that all Russian vowels tend to have a less distinct enunciation when unstressed than when stressed; this is particularly noticeable in the case of a and o, which have practically the sound of the when unstressed (they are clearer in the syllable immediately preceding the stressed syllable).

Consonant Sounds

б, в, д, з, к, л, м, н, п, т, ф, approximately like English b, v, d, z, k, l, m, n, p, t, f, respectively.[*]

---

[*] Russian consonants, however, tend to become palatalized when followed by vowels containing the *y*-sound as their first element (е, ё, и, ь, ю, я). In many cases the palatalization is instinctive for an English speaker; thus, в followed by a "hard" vowel (а, о, у, ы, э) will naturally assume the sound of in*v*oke, while if it is followed by a "soft" vowel (е, ё, и, ь, ю, я) it will naturally assume the sound of *view*; б will be pronounced as in *booty* or as in *beauty*, respectively; п as in *pat* or in *pure*, etc. In the case of т, д, л, н, the "soft" pronunciation, when one of the "soft" vowels follows, will go as far as hi*t you*, di*d you*, mi*llio*n, o*nio*n, respectively (теперь, now; делать, to do; любовь, love; день, day).

г = *go*: много, much, many;●

ж = *measure*: жена, wife;

р = British ve*r*y: Россия, Russia;

с = *so*, in *all* positions: соус, sauce;

х = German a*ch*: храбрый, brave; худой, bad;

ц = *its*: церковь, church;

ч = *ch*ill: чёрный, black;

ш = *sure*: шесть, six;

щ = A *h-h*urch; борщ, beet soup; щека, cheek; женщина, woman.

There is no rule for Russian accentuation, and the place of the accent is not ordinarily indicated in writing. The stress may fall on *any* syllable, and each word must be learned with its own stress; furthermore, the stress *in the same word* often changes position according to the case form used (мужик, peasant; but мужика, of the peasant), and from the singular to the plural (вода, water; but воды, waters). While a misplaced accent is not an unforgivable crime, some care should be taken to avoid too many wrong accentuations, since an error in stress sometimes leads to a change in meaning.

● Final *voiced* consonants (б, в, г, д, з, ж) tend to assume the corresponding *unvoiced* pronunciation (p, f, k, t, s, sh); thus, зуб, tooth, is pronounced *zoop*; Романов (a family name), *Románof*; друг, friend, *drook*; дед, grandfather, *dyet*; раз, time, *ras*; муж, husband, *moosh*.

11

PART
I

GRAMMATICAL COURSE

GRAMMAR

Nouns

Russian has no article, definite or indefinite; друг means "friend," "a friend," "the friend."

There are three genders, masculine, feminine and neuter; but inanimate objects are often masculine or feminine. The ending generally helps to determine the gender of a noun. Nouns ending in consonants or -й (and some ending in -ь) are masculine, those ending in -a or -я (and most of those ending in -ь) feminine, those in -о, -е or -мя neuter.

Russian has six cases: nominative, genitive, dative, accusative, instrumental, and locative or prepositional (a separate vocative appears in a few words only, and need not be considered). These cases and their endings are alive, and have to be reckoned with; while an occasional error in case or ending is forgivable, too many such errors will make the language incomprehensible to the native.

There are numerous declensional schemes, but the following are the most common. The endings are given in the order indicated above.

Masculine Nouns

Singular: —, -a, -y, -a or —,* -ом, -е;
Plural: -ы, -ов, -ам, -ов or -ы,* -ами, -ах.
　(Decline thus: офицер, офицера, etc., officer; стол, стола, etc., table; отец, отца, etc., father).
Singular: -й, -я, -ю, -я or -й, -ем, -е;
Plural: -и, -ев, -ям, -ев or -и, -ями, -ях.
　(Decline thus: герой, героя, etc., hero).
Singular: -ь, -я, -ю, -я or -ь, -ем, -е;
Plural: -и, -ей, -ям, -ей or -и, -ями, -ях.
　Decline thus: приятель, приятеля, etc., friend; рубль, рубля, etc., ruble).

---

* Masculine nouns in both singular and plural, and feminine nouns in the *plural only*, make their accusative form coincide with the genitive if a living person or animal is denoted, with the nominative if an inanimate object appears; thus, the accusative of офицер and отец is офицера and отца, respectively; but the accusative of стол is стол.

15

FEMININE NOUNS

Singular: -а, -ы, -е, -у, -ою (-ой), -е;
Plural: -ы, —, -ам, — or -ы, -ами, -ах.

(Decline thus: женщина, женщины, etc., woman; война, войны, etc.; plural войны, etc., war).

Singular: -я, -и, -е, -ю, -ею (-ей), -е (if nominative has и before я, dative and prepositional have -и instead of -е);
Plural: -и, -ь, -ям, -ь or -и, -ями, -ях.

(Decline thus: пустыня, пустыни, etc., desert; Россия, Russia).

Singular: -ь, -и, -и, -ь, -ью, -и;
Plural: -и, -ей, -ям, -ей or -и, -ями, -ях.

(Decline thus: постель, постели, etc., bed; дверь, двери, etc.; plural двери, but дверей, дверям, etc., door).

NEUTER NOUNS

Singular: -о, -а, -у, -о, -ом, -е;
Plural: -а, —, -ам, -а, -ами, -ах.

(Decline thus: масло, масла, etc., butter; место, места, etc., plural места, etc., place; село, села, etc., plural сёла, etc., village).

Singular: -е, -я, -ю, -е, -ем, -е (-и if nom. ends in -ие);
Plural: -я, -ей (-ий if nom. sg. ends in -ие), -ям, -я, -ями, -ях.

(Decline thus: море, моря, etc., plural моря, etc., sea; поле, поля, etc.; plural поля, etc., field; здание, здания, etc., building).

Singular: -мя, -мени, -мени, -мя, -менем, -мени;
Plural: -мена, -мен, -менам, -мена, -менами, -менах.

(Decline thus: время, времени, etc.; plural времена, времён, etc., time; имя, имени, etc.; plural имена, имён, etc., name).

These schemes are perhaps less complicated than they appear at first glance. Note that in neuter nouns, and in masculine nouns denoting inanimate objects, the accusative has the same form as the nominative, while in masculine nouns denoting living things it has the same form as the genitive; note also the almost invariable -ом, -ем of the instrumental singular, the -е of the prepositional singular, the -ам or -ям of the dative plural, the -ами or -ями of the instrumental plural, and the -ах or -ях of the prepositional plural. Note also that in neuter nouns the accent of the plural is usually on a different syllable from that of the singular.

Adjectives and Adverbs

Adjectives agree in number, gender and *case* with the nouns they modify. The following is the most common scheme of adjective declension:

	Singular			Plural
	Masc.	Fem.	Neut.	(all genders)
Nom.	-ый	-ая	-ое	-ые
Gen.	-ого*	-ой	-ого	-ых
Dat.	-ому	-ой	-ому	-ым
Acc.	-ого or -ый	-ую	-ое	Genitive or Nominative, according as the noun is living or inanimate
Instr.	-ым	-ой (-ою)	-ым	-ыми
Loc.	-ом	-ой	-ом	-ых

(Decline thus: старый, old; трудный, difficult.)

Two common variants of this scheme are: -ий, -яя, -ее (the "hard" vowel changes to the corresponding "soft" one throughout: а becomes я, ы becomes и, о becomes ё, у becomes ю; decline thus: ранний, early); and -ой, -ая, -ое, genitive -ого, -ой, -ого, etc., like the -ый type, save that the stress is on the ending (decline thus: простой, simple).**

If the adjective is used as a predicate adjective after the verb "to be" (and similar verbs, like "to seem," etc.), it assumes the following forms: masc. sg., —; fem. sg. -а; neut. sg., -о; plural (all genders), -ы: стар, стара, старо, plural стары, old; труден, трудна, трудно, plural трудны, difficult; прост, проста, просто, plural просты, simple. The verb "to be" in the present tense is omitted: она—стара, she is old.

---

* In the genitive endings -го, -его, -ого of adjectives and pronouns, the г is always pronounced as *v*.

** If the adjective root ends in г, ж, к, х, ч, ц, щ, the following replacements must be made: и for ы, а for я, у for ю; if it ends in ц, я and ю must be replaced by а, у; if it ends in ж, ц, ч, ш, щ, о must be replaced by е; thus, великий, великая, великое, great; горячий, горячая, горячее, hot. These replacements appear not only in adjectives, but in nouns, pronouns and verbs as well.

The comparative degree is generally formed by changing the ending of the adjective to -ee, which is not declined: красивый, beautiful; красивее, more beautiful; умный, intelligent; умнее, more intelligent. "Than" is expressed by чем with the nominative, or, more frequently, by the genitive without чем: он умнее чем я, or он умнее меня, he is more intelligent than I; железо полезнее чем серебро, or железо полезнее серебра, iron is more useful than silver. If the verb "to be" is not involved, the comparative is more usually formed by prefixing более (more) to the positive: более красивый стул, a more beautiful chair.

The superlative, both relative and absolute, is usually formed by prefixing самый to the positive: самый умный the most intelligent, extremely intelligent.

The adverb generally consists of the neuter predicate form of the adjective: хороший, good; хорошо, well; умный, intelligent; умно, intelligently; жаркий, warm; жарко, warmly.

Pronouns

PERSONAL

"I," "of me," "to me," etc.—я, меня, мне, меня, мною or мной, мне.

"you" (familiar), "of you," etc.—ты, тебя, тебе, тебя, тобою or тобой, тебе.

"he," "his," etc.—он, (н)его, (н)ему, (н)его, (н)им, нём.[*]

"she," "her," etc.—она, (н)ея, (н)ей, (н)её, (н)ею, ней.

"it," "its," etc.—оно, (н)его, (н)ему, (н)его, (н)им, нём.

"we," "of us," "to us," etc.—мы, нас, нам, нас, нами, нас.

"you" (fam. pl. and polite sg. or pl.)—вы, вас, вам, вас, вами, вас.

"they"—они, (н)их, (н)им, (н)их, (н)ми, (н)их.

"self," "oneself"—(no nom.), себя, себе, себя, собою or собой, себе.

---

[*] The forms его, него; ему, нему, etc., are *not* interchangeable; use forms with н- when the pronoun is governed by a preposition: у него хлеб, he has bread; but у его отца хлеб, his father has bread.

18

POSSESSIVE

"my," "mine" (masc. and neut.)—мой (neut. моё), моего, моему, nom. or gen., моим, моём; (fem.)—моя, моей, моей, мою, моею or моей, моей; (plural, all genders)—мои, моих, моим, мои or моих, моими, моих.

Твой, "your," "yours" (fam.), and свой, one's own, are declined in the same fashion. Наш (наша, наше), "our," "ours," and ваш (ваша, ваше), "your," "yours," are similarly declined, but with the accent always on the root. For "his," "her," "its," "their," use the genitive of the personal pronoun: его, of him (his); её, of her (her, hers); его, of it, (its); их, of them (their, theirs).

DEMONSTRATIVE

this, these—этот (neut. это), этого, этому, (gen. or nom.), этим, этом; Fem.—эта, этой, этой, эту, этой, этой; Plural—эти, этих, этим, эти or этих, этими, этих.

that, those—тот (neut. то), того, тому, (nom. or gen.), тем, том; Fem.—та, той, той, ту, той, той; Plural—те, тех, тем, те or тех, теми, тех.

RELATIVE AND INTERROGATIVE

who, which, that—который (fully declined as a regular adjective; may also be used as an interrogative);

who?, whose?, to whom?, whom?—кто, кого, кому, кого, кем, ком (may also be used as a relative);

what?, which?—что, чего, чему, что, чем, чём (may also be used as a relative);

whose?—чей (fem. чья; neut. чьё; declined like мой);

what sort of?—какой (declined as a regular adjective).

Verbs

The Russian verb has only three tenses: present, past and future. On the other hand, most verbs have a double "aspect": the "imperfective," indicating an action that is, was, or will be going on, and the "perfective," denoting an action that happened once and was completed, or that will be begun and completed;

19

the imperfective verb is usually a simple verb, the perfective verb often (but not always) has a preposition prefixed to it (писать, to be writing; написать, to write once). The perfective verb, by its nature, cannot have a present tense, but only a past (action that was begun and finished) and a future (action that will be begun and finished); and while the past of a perfective verb is quite similar in form to the past of an imperfective verb, the perfective *future* has a set of endings similar to those of the *present* of an imperfective verb; or, to word it differently, the present *form* of the perfective verb has a future *meaning*. Thus, писать, to be writing, has a present, пишу (I am writing); a past, писал (I was writing, I used to write); and a future, буду писать (I shall be writing); but написать, the perfective counterpart of the imperfective писать, has only a past, написал (I wrote once, and finished writing); and a future with present form, напишу (I shall write once, and be finished).

The infinitive of Russian verbs usually ends in -ть (a certain number of verbs have -чь or -ти): делать, to do; говорить, to speak; ежчь, to burn; нести, to carry. Its use is similar to that of the English infinitive: я хочу говорить, I wish to speak.

PRESENT INDICATIVE

The normal endings are: -у (or -ю), -ешь, -ет, -ем, -ете, -ут (or -ют); or: -у (-ю), -ишь, -ит, -им, -ите, -ат (-ят).

I do, дела-ю	I speak, говор-ю
you do, дела-ешь [10]	you speak, говор-ишь ●
he does, дела-ет	he speaks, говор-ит
we do, дела-ем	we speak, говор-им
you do, дела-ете [10]	you speak, говор-ите ●
they do, дела-ют	they speak, говор-ят

There are many deviations from these two fundamental schemes; нести and verbs of its type have: несу, несёшь, несёт, etc.; several verbs in -ть, with stress on the last vowel, follow this scheme (жить, to live, has живу, живёшь, живёт, etc.).

Note carefully that the *future* of perfective verbs has precisely the same form and endings as the *present* of imperfective verbs; thus, написать to write (once, and be through writing), has no present, while its future (I shall write once, and be through) runs: напишу, напишешь, напишет, etc.

● The second person singular is used only in intimate conversation; the second plural is regularly used in addressing a single person politely, and in addressing more than one person, familiarly or politely. The subject pronoun is generally used, but is sometimes omitted.

The verb "to be," быть, has an archaic present as follows: есмь, еси, есть, есмы, есте, суть. These forms, however, are not used in modern Russian (я—болен, I am ill); the third person singular only is regularly used in interrogative sentences expressing possession: есть ли у вас рубль?, have you a ruble? (lit. is there by you a ruble?).

PAST INDICATIVE

This tense is formed by adding to the stem of the verb the endings -л, -ла, -ло, according to the *gender* of the subject (-ли in the plural, for all genders). This so-called past tense is really only a past participle, with predicate adjective endings, and agreement in gender and number with the subject.

I spoke, я говори-л (fem. говори-ла)
you spoke, ты говори-л (fem. говори-ла)
he spoke, он говори-л
she spoke, она говори-ла
we spoke, мы говори-ли
you spoke, вы говори-ли
they spoke, они говори-ли

Note that this tense functions as an imperfect (I was doing, used to do) in the case of imperfective verbs; but as a past, present perfect or past perfect in the case of perfective verbs: я писал, I was writing, used to write; я написал, I wrote, have written, had written.

The past tense of быть is был (была, было, plural были). It is regularly used, not omitted as is the case with the present: я был болен, I was ill.

FUTURE

For the future of perfective verbs, see under Present Tense. The future of imperfective verbs is formed by using the future of быть (to be), followed by the infinitive:

I shall speak, я буду говорить
you will speak, ты будешь говорить
he will speak, он будет говорить
she will speak, она будет говорить
we shall speak, мы будем говорить
you will speak, вы будете говорить
they will speak, они будут говорить

The future of perfective verbs does service for our future perfect.

The conditional idea (should, would) is normally expressed by the past tense of the verb followed by the particle бы: он делал бы, he would do, he would have done. Если бы он был здесь, мы могли бы вместе работать, if he were (had been) here, we could work (could have worked) together.

The subjunctive idea is generally rendered by the past tense introduced by чтобы: он написал, чтобы он купил сад, he wrote in order that he might buy the garden. Я хочу, чтобы он объяснил нам, I wish he would explain to us.

IMPERATIVE

The imperative generally ends in -й, -и, -ь (singular), and -йте, -ите, -ьте (plural): сделай, сделайте, do!; говори, говорите, speak!; неси, несите, carry!; будь, будьте, be!

PARTICIPLES AND GERUNDS

Russian has two indeclinable gerunds, present and past: говоря, by or while speaking; поговорив, or поговоривши, having spoken.

There are four participles declined like adjectives: present active, говорящий, speaking; present passive, делаемый, being done; past active, говоривший, having spoken; past passive, читанный, having been read.

The use of gerunds and participles is quite complicated, and all the forms given above do not appear for all verbs. Generally speaking, they are very frequently used where other languages would use a subordinate clause (сказанное слово, the word that was spoken).

PASSIVE AND REFLEXIVE

There is no true passive in Russian, save for the participial forms above indicated. The passive concept is generally rendered: (1) by a passive participle; (2) by an indefinite third person plural active (мне сказали, I was told; lit. they told me); (3) by the reflexive (это делается, this is being done, lit. this does itself).

Reflexive verbs are quite numerous. They are formed, for all persons, by the addition of -ся (an abbreviated form of себя; -сь after vowels, except ь): умываться, to wash oneself: я умываюсь, ты умываешься, он умывается, мы умываемся, вы умываетесь, они умываются; past: я умывался (fem. я умывалась; pl. мы умывались); fut.: я буду умываться.

The Preposition в	The Preposition на
в институ́те	на ку́рсе
в университе́те	на факульте́те
в кла́ссе	на уро́ке
в гру́ппе	на экза́мене
	на ле́кции
в магази́не	на фа́брике
	на заво́де
	на по́чте
	на вокза́ле
в клу́бе	на ве́чере
	на собра́нии
	на ми́тинге
в музе́е	на экску́рсии
	на вы́ставке
в теа́тре	на бале́те
в го́роде	на у́лице
	на пло́щади
	на стадио́не
	на ю́ге
	на се́вере
	на за́паде
	на восто́ке
в стране́	на ро́дине

NOTES ON THE USE OF THE CASES

The nominative is the case of the subject; it is also used in the predicate nominative, after the verb "to be" (the latter is generally understood, not expressed, in the present tense): ваш сын—не маленький мальчик, your son is not a young boy; где ваш отец?, where is your father?

The genitive expresses possession: дом моего брата, the house of my brother, my brother's house. To translate the English "to have" in the sense of "to own," Russian generally uses the preposition у with the genitive case: у меня—большой дом, I have a large house (literally, by me [is] a large house); есть ли у мальчика хлеб?, has the boy the bread? (literally, is by the boy the bread?; ли is an untranslatable interrogative particle often used in questions, but only when no other interrogative word appears). The genitive is regularly used in negative sentences, replacing the accusative: я не знал дома, I didn't know the house; у меня—нет хлеба, I have no bread (literally, by me [is] not of bread). It is used to translate "some," "any" (дайте мне хлеба, give me bread, some bread; as against дайте мне хлеб, give me *the* bread); and after adverbs of quantity (много хлеба, lots of bread, literally, much of bread). It appears with several prepositions, chief among them the у mentioned above; без, without (без книги, without a book); для, for, for the sake of (для меня, for me, for my sake); из, from, out of (из России, out of Russia); от, away from (especially a person: от моего друга, from my friend).

The dative indicates the indirect object after verbs of saying, giving, etc.: я дал мальчику хлеб, I gave the boy the bread. It is also used after certain prepositions, chief among them к (ко before troublesome consonant groups), toward: к мальчику, toward the boy; ко мне, toward me, to my house.

The accusative is the case of the direct object. Note that a separate accusative form appears only in the feminine singular; in the masculine and neuter singular, and in all plurals, the accusative takes the form of the nominative for inanimate objects, of the genitive for living persons and animals. It is also used with certain prepositions after verbs of motion, particularly в (во), in, into; на, on, onto, upon; за, behind. Note that several of these prepositions take the accusative if motion is involved, but the locative or instrumental if no idea of motion appears: он пошёл в город (acc.), he went into the city; but он был в городе (loc.), he was in the city; он сел на стул, he sat down on the chair (acc.), but он сидел на стуле, he was sitting on the chair (loc.).

The instrumental denotes means or instrument (with, by means of): он писал карандашом, he was writing with a pencil. It is used with several prepositions, notably с (со), with, in company with: с офицером, with the officer; со мною, with me; за, behind; перед, in front of. It also appears idiomatically in certain expressions of time: завтра утром, tomorrow morning.

The locative or prepositional is *always* used with prepositions, and frequently denotes place where or in which (*not* place to which; the accusative denotes that): о (об, обо), about: о тебе, about you; об офицере, about the officer; обо мне, about me; на, on, upon: на столе, on the table; в (во), in: в городе, in the city; во мне, within me.

Numerals

CARDINAL

Outside of один, one, these are treated as nouns, are fully declined, and are followed by the *genitive* of the noun to which they refer (genitive *singular* after 2, 3, 4; genitive *plural* after all others): один дом, one house; два дома, two houses; пять домов, five houses. Один, одна, одно, plural одни (meaning "alone," "some"), is otherwise declined like этот (see p. 144), but with the accent on the ending. Два, fem. две, has gen. двух, dat. двум, instr. двумя, loc. двух; три has трёх, трём, тремя, трёх; четыре has -ёх, -ём, -ьмя, -ёх. Numerals ending in -ь are declined like feminine nouns in -ь; others are declined like nouns of the corresponding classes, according to their endings.

1 = один (одна, одно)	12 = двенадцать
2 = два (две, два)	13 = тринадцать
3 = три	14 = четырнадцать
4 = четыре	15 = пятнадцать
5 = пять	16 = шестнадцать
6 = шесть	17 = семнадцать
7 = семь	18 = восемнадцать
8 = восемь	19 = девятнадцать
9 = девять	20 = двадцать
10 = десять	21 = двадцать один
11 = одиннадцать	

30 = тридцать	400 = четыреста
40 = сорок	500 = пятьсот
50 = пятьдесят	600 = шестьсот
60 = шестьдесят	1000 = тысяча
70 = семьдесят	2000 = две тысячи
80 = восемьдесят	5000 = пять тысяч
90 = девяносто	1,000,000 = миллион
100 = сто	7635 = семь тысяч
200 = двести	шестьсот тридцать
300 = триста	пять

ORDINAL (declined like ordinary adjectives)

1st = первый	20th = двадцатый
2nd = второй	21st = двадцать первый
3rd = третий	30th = тридцатый
4th = четвёртый	40th = сороковой
5th = пятый	50th = пятидесятый
6th = шестой	60th = шестидесятый
7th = седьмой	70th = семидесятый
8th = восьмой	80th = восьмидесятый
9th = девятый	90th = девяностый
10th = десятый	100th = сотый
11th = одиннадцатый	145th = сто сорок пятый

Use these in dates, either in the genitive, or in the neuter nominative: десятого мая or десятое мая, May 10th.

Once—раз; twice—два раза; five times—пять раз; the first time—первый раз; every time—каждый раз; the last time—последний раз.

EXERCISES

Exercise 1. Answer the questions.

1. Когда́ вы обе́даете, днём и́ли ве́чером?
2. Когда́ вы у́жинаете, ве́чером и́ли днём?
3. Когда́ вы слу́шаете ра́дио, у́тром и́ли ве́чером?
4. Когда́ ты рабо́таешь, днём и́ли ве́чером?
5. Когда́ ты отдыха́ешь, днём и́ли ве́чером?
6. Когда́ ты чита́ешь газе́ты, у́тром и́ли ве́чером?
7. Когда́ ты занима́ешься , днём и́ли ве́чером?

Exercise 2. Answer the questions.

1. Что де́лает Андре́й у́тром?
2. Что он де́лает днём?
3. Что де́лают студе́нты сейча́с?
4. Что они́ де́лают ве́чером?
5. Что вы де́лаете сейча́с?
6. Что вы де́лаете у́тром?
7. Что вы де́лаете ве́чером?
8. Что де́лает Андре́й по́сле обе́да? [1]
9. Что вы де́лаете по́сле уро́ка?
10. Что де́лают студе́нты по́сле у́жина?
11. Что де́лает Андре́й по́сле за́втрака?
12. Что де́лает Ни́на по́сле уро́ка?

Exercise 3. Answer the questions

1. — *Как* студе́нтка отвеча́ет уро́к?
   — Студе́нтка отвеча́ет уро́к *пра́вильно*.
2. — *Как* Ви́ктор чита́ет?
   — Ви́ктор чита́ет *гро́мко*.
3. — *Как* студе́нты [1] слу́шают?
   — Студе́нты слу́шают *внима́тельно*.
4. — *Как* Анна зна́ет текст?
   — Анна зна́ет текст *хорошо́*.

Exercise 4. Answer the questions using the words
given in brackets.

1. Кто читáет текст? (Анна)
2. Кто хорошó читáет текст? (Анна и Пáвел)
3. Кто сейчáс повторя́ет текст? (они́)
4. Кто знáет диалóг? (я)
5. Кто хорошó знáет диалóг? (студéнт и студéнтка)
6. Кто говори́т по-ру́сски? (они́)
7. Кто хорошó говори́т по-ру́сски? (вы)
8. Кто сейчáс говори́т по-ру́сски? (мы)
9. Кто изучáет англи́йский язы́к? (онá)

Exercise 5. Read the questions and answers
and write them down.

1. Кто э́то?
   Это Ви́ктор.
   Кто он?
   Он студéнт.
   Он слу́шает рáдио?
   Нет, он читáет письмó.

2. Это Бори́с?
   Да, э́то Бори́с.
   Он студéнт?
   Да, он студéнт.
   Он читáет журнáл?
   Да, он читáет журнáл.

Exercise 6. Answer the questions.

1. Где у́чится ваш друг?
   Что нахóдится на э́той у́лице?
   О чём расскáзывал ваш друг?
   Что вы ви́дите спрáва?
2. Что вы читáете?
   Где лежи́т письмó?
   Что лежи́т на столé?
   О чём вы говори́те?
3. Кто сиди́т в аудитóрии?
   Когó спрáшивает профéссор?
   О ком вы говори́те?

Exercise 7. Answer the questions.

A. 1. Куда́ вы положи́ли мою́ кни́гу?
    2. Куда́ он положи́л ва́шу ру́чку?
    3. Куда́ ты положи́л мой каранда́ш?
    4. Куда́ она́ положи́ла свою́ па́пку?
    5. Куда́ они́ положи́ли свои́ тетра́ди?
    6. Куда́ он кладёт свой портфе́ль?
    7. Куда́ вы кладёте свои́ ве́щи?
    8. Куда́ вы кладёте де́ньги?
B. 1. Куда́ он поста́вил цветы́?
    2. Куда́ он поста́вил чемода́н?
    3. Куда́ мы ста́вим цветы́?
    4. Куда́ мы ста́вим кни́ги?
C. 1. Куда́ вы пове́сили карти́ну?
    2. Куда́ ты хо́чешь пове́сить э́ту фотогра́фию?
    3. Куда́ она́ пове́сила пла́тье?
    4. Куда́ вы ве́шаете костю́мы?

Exercise 8. Answer the questions.

A. 1. Кому́ вы написа́ли письмо́ вчера́?
    2. Кому́ вы рассказа́ли о ве́чере?
    3. Кому́ вы купи́ли газе́ту?
    4. Кому́ студе́нты отвеча́ют на экза́мене?
    5. Кому́ студе́нты пока́зывают тетра́ди?
    6. Кому́ вы рассказа́ли о свое́й боле́зни?
B. 7. Кому́ преподава́тель объясни́л но́вые слова́?
    8. Кому́ Оле́г посла́л свои́ но́вые фотогра́фии?
    9. Кому́ он купи́л пода́рок?
   10. Кому́ оте́ц подари́л кни́гу?

Exercise 9. Answer the questions using the words given on the right.

1. Кого́ вы спроси́ли об экза́менах? Кому́ вы сказа́ли об экза́менах?	наш преподава́тель
2. Кого́ вы пригласи́ли на ве́чер? Кому́ вы да́ли биле́т на ве́чер?	мой ста́рый друг
3. Кого́ вы попроси́ли купи́ть биле́ты в теа́тр? Кому́ вы обеща́ли купи́ть биле́ты в теа́тр?	знако́мый студе́нт
4. Кого́ вы поблагодари́ли за кни́гу? Кому́ вы сказа́ли «спаси́бо» за кни́гу?	наш библиоте́карь
5. Кого́ вы спроси́ли, где нахо́дится университе́т? Кому́ вы объясни́ли, где нахо́дится университе́т?	оди́н незнако́мый челове́к
6. Кого́ вы поздра́вили с Но́вым го́дом? [1] Кому́ вы посла́ли поздравле́ние?	мои́ роди́тели и друзья́
7. Кого́ вы давно́ не ви́дели? Кому́ вы пе́редали приве́т? О ком вы ду́мали вчера́?	мои́ ста́рые друзья́ и това́рищи
8. Кого́ вы ча́сто вспомина́ете? Кому́ вы ча́сто пи́шете пи́сьма? О ком вы ча́сто ду́маете?	оте́ц и мать, бра́тья и сёстры

Exercise 10. Answer the questions

1. Кому́ профе́ссор чита́ет ле́кцию?
2. Кому́ вы сообщи́ли о собра́нии?
3. Кому́ вы купи́ли пода́рки?
4. Кому́ вы звони́ли сего́дня?
5. Кому́ Бори́с посла́л свои́ фотогра́фии?
6. Кому́ мать купи́ла велосипе́д?
7. Кому́ помога́ет Анна?
8. Како́й студе́нтке вы помога́ете изуча́ть ру́сский язы́к?

31

Exercise 11. Answer the questions

1. Какой экзамен вы будете сдавать завтра?
2. Какую лекцию вы слушали вчера?
3. Какой учебник вам надо купить?
4. Какую тетрадь вы потеряли?
5. Какую книгу вам надо взять в библиотеке?
6. Какую контрольную работу вы писали сегодня?
7. Какая консультация будет завтра?

Exercise 12. Insert the words given on the right.

1. Он давно не видел . . . .
   Вчера он приезжал . . . .
   Он вошёл и поздоровался . . . .

   я и мои товарищи

2. Недавно я получил письмо . . . .
   Вчера я встречал на вокзале . . . .
   Я хочу познакомить вас . . . .

   мои родители

3. Мне очень нравятся . . . .
   Вчера в клубе мы видели . . . .
   После концерта мы разговаривали . . . .

   эти молодые артисты

4. Я очень люблю . . .
   Я часто пишу письма . . . .
   Я часто получаю письма . . . .
   Я всегда советуюсь . . . .

   мой старший брат

5. Вчера на улице я встретил . . . .
   Я поздоровался . . . .
   Павел помогает изучать русский язык . . . .
   Сегодня на уроке не было . . . .
   Этот журнал дала мне . . . .

   наша новая студентка

32

PART
II

CONVERSATIONAL
EXPRESSIONS

1

GREETINGS, ETIQUETTE, SOCIAL AMENITIES

Good morning.
Доброе утро.
DAW-bruh-yeh OO-truh.

Good afternoon.
Добрый день.
DAW-bry d'ehn'.

Good-by.
Прощайте.
pruhsh-CHEYE-t'eh.

Till we meet again.
До свиданья.
duh sv'i-DAH-n'uh.

See you later (tonight, tomorrow).
Увижу вас позднее (вечером, завтра).
oo-V'EE-zhoo vahs puhz-DN'EH-yeh (V'EH-chi-ruhm, ZAHF-truh).

Hello!
Алло!
uh-LAW!

How are you? How do you do?
Как вы поживаете?
kahk vy puh-zhy-VAH-yi-t'eh?

How are things?
Как дела?
kahk d'i-LAH?

I'm well (much better), thank you.
Благодарю вас, хорошо (много лучше).
bluh-guh-duh-R'OO vahs, khuh-ruh-SHAW (MNAW-guh LOOCH-sheh).

Good evening.
Добрый вечер.
DAW-bry V'EH-chuhr.

Good night.
Спокойной ночи.
spuh-KOI-noi NAW-chi.

It's nothing.
Это ничего.
EH-tuh n'i-chi-VAW.

I'm glad.
Я рад (рада).
yah raht (RAH-duh).

Is it not so?
Не правда ли?
n'i PRAHV-duh l'i?

Yes.
Да.
dah.

No.
Нет.
n'cht.

Please.
Пожалуйста.
puh-ZHAHL-stuh.

Perhaps.
Может быть.
MAW-zhyt byt'.

Thank you.
Спасибо (благодарю вас).
spuh-S'EE-buh (bluh-guh-duh-R'OO vahs).

Don't mention it (you're welcome).
Не за что (пожалуйста).
N'EH-zuh-shtuh (puh-ZHAHL-stuh).

Pardon me.
Простите (извините).
pruh-ST'EE-t'eh (eez-v'i-N'EE-t'eh).

It doesn't matter.
Это не важно (*or* ничего).
EH-tuh n'i VAHZH-nuh (n'i-chi-VAW).

I'm sorry.
Сожалею (*or* виноват).
suh-zhuh-L'EH-yoo (v'i-nuh-VAHT).

I(can't) think so.
Я (не) думаю что так.
yah (n'i) DOO-muh-yoo shtaw tahk.

You're right (wrong).
Вы правы (ошибаетесь).
vy pruh-VY (uh-shy-BAH-yi-t'ehs').

Not at all.
Совсем нет.
suhv-S'EHM n'cht.

I agree.
Я согласен (согласна).
yah suh-GLAH-s'in (suh-GLAHS-nuh).

It's all right.
Это хорошо.
EH-tuh khuh-ruh-SHAW.

O.K.
Хорошо.
khuh-ruh-SHAW.

Do you like ——?
Нравится ли вам ——?
NRAH-v'it-suh l'i vahm ——?

Would you like ——?
Хотите ли вы ——?
khuh-T'EE-t'eh l'i vy ——?

Do you want ——?
Хотите ——?
khuh-T'EE-t'eh ——?

Help yourself.
Берите, пожалуйста.
b'i-R'EE-t'eh, puh-ZHAHL-stuh.

To your health!
За ваше здоровье!
zuh VAH-sheh zduh-RAW-v'eh!

To yours!
За ваше!
zuh VAH-sheh!

Congratulations!
Поздравляю!
puhz-druhv-L'AH-yoo!

Best wishes!
Наилучшие пожелания!
neye-LOOCH-shy-yeh puh-zhy-LAH-n'i-yuh!

Merry Christmas!
С праздником Рождества Христова!
SPRAHZ-dn'i-kuhm ruhzh-d'ist-VAH khr'is-TAW-vuh!

Happy New Year!
Счастливого Нового Года!
schuhst-L'EE-vuh-vuh NAW-vuh-vuh GAW-duh!

Certainly.
Действительно.
d'eyst-V'EE-t'il'-nuh.

As you wish.
Как хотите.
kahk khuh-T'EE-t'eh.

Of course.
Конечно.
kuh-N'EHCH-nuh.

Gladly.
Охотно.
uh-KHAWT-nuh.

As quickly as possible.
Как можно скорее.
kahk MAWZH-nuh skuh-R'EH-yeh.

How long have you been waiting?
Как долго (or сколько времени) вы ждёте?
kahk DAWL-guh (SKAWL'-kuh VR'EH-m'i-n'i) vy ZHD'AW-t'eh?

Sorry to keep you waiting.
Простите, что заставил вас ждать.
pruh-ST'EE-t'eh, shtaw zuh-STAH-v'il (zuh-STAH-v'i-luh) vahs zhdaht'.

You have been very kind.
Вы очень добры.
vy AW-chin' duh-BRY.

I am most grateful.
Премного благодарен (благодарна).
pr'im-NAW-guh bluh-guh-DAH-r'in (bluh-guh-DAHR-nuh).

A pleasant journey!
Счастливого пути!
schuhst-L'EE-vuh-vuh poo-T'EE!

A pleasant stay!
Приятного времяпрепровождения!
pr'i-YAHT-nuh-vuh vr'i-m'uh-pr'i-pruh-vuhzh-D'EH-n'i-yuh!

Glad to meet you!
Рад (рада) с вами познакомиться! (or Очень приятно!)
raht (RAH-duh) SVAH-m'i puhz-nuh-KAW-m'it'-suh! (AW-chin' pr'i-YAHT-nuh!)

38

The pleasure is mine!
Очень приятно!
AW-chin' pr'i-YAHT-nuh!

Please sit down.
Садитесь пожалуйста.
suh-D'EE-t'ehs' puh-ZHAHL-stuh.

Make yourself at home.
Чувствуйте себя как дома.
CHOOFS-tvooy-t'eh s'i-B'AH kahk DAW-muh.

Give my regards to ——.
Передайте мой привет ——.
p'i-r'i-DEYE-t'eh moi pr'i-V'EHT ——.

In any case, let me hear from you.
Во всяком случае дайте о себе знать.
vuh FS'AH-kuhm SLOO-chuh-yeh DEYE-t'eh uh s'i-B'I
znaht'.

May I introduce my friend.
Позвольте представить вам моего друга.
puhz-VAWL'-t'eh   pr'id-STAH-v'it'   vahm   muh-yi-VA'
DROO-guh.

my wife мою жену muh-YOO zhy-NOO

my husband моего мужа muh-yi-VAW MOO-zhuh

my son моего сына muh-yi-VAW SY-nuh

my daughter мою дочь muh-YOO dawch'

my sister мою сестру muh-YOO s'is-TROO

my brother моего брата muh-yi-VAW BRAH-tuh

my father моего отца muh-yi-VAW uh-TSAH

my mother мою мать muh-YOO maht'

my uncle моего дядю muh-yi-VAW D'AH-d'oo

my aunt мою тётку muh-YOO T'AWT-koo

2

EXCLAMATIONS, COLLOQUIALISMS

What a pity!
Как жаль!
kahk zhahl'!

Too bad!
К сожалению!
ksuh-zhuh-L'EH-n'i-yoo!

For Heaven's sake!
Ради Бога!
RAH-d'ee BAW-guh!

Nonsense!
Ерунда!
yi-roon-DAH!

Darn it!
Чорт возьми!
CHAWRT vuhz'-M'EE!

What a guy!
Ну и дядя!
noo ee D'AH-d'uh!

Gangway!
Посторонитесь! (*or* дорогу!)
puh-stuh-ruh-N'EE-t'ehs'! (duh-RAW-goo!)

That's fine!
Чудно! (*or* Хорошо!)
CHOOD-nuh! (khuh-ruh-SHAW!)

That's enough!
Довольно!
duh-VAWL'-nuh!

Never mind!
Ничего!
n'i-chi-VAW!

You don't say so!
Неужели!
n'i-oo-ZHEH-l'ee!

Honest!
Честное слово?
CHEST-nuh-yeh SLAW-vuh?

What an awful dump!
Какая ужасная дыра!
kuh-KAH-yuh oo-ZHAHS-nuh-yuh dy-RAH!

That's swell!
Это здорово!
EH-tuh ZDAW-ruh-vuh!

Scram!
Вон!
vawn!

Good luck!
Желаю счастья!
zhy-LAH-yoo SCHAHS-t'uh!

What the devil!
Что за чёрт!
shtaw zuh CHAWRT!

Ouch!
Ой!
oi!

Hell!
Чорт возьми!
CHAWRT vuhz-M'EE!

Go to the devil!
Иди к чорту!
ee-D'EE KCHAWR-too!

You bet!
А что вы думаете! (*or* конечно!)
uh shtaw vy DOO-muh-yi-t'eh! (kuh-N'EHCH-nuh!)

You bet I did!
Конечно я сделал!
kuh-N'EHCH-nuh yah SD'EH-luhl!

What nerve!
Какая дерзость!
kuh-KAH-yuh D'EHR-zuhst'!

He's a louse (dumbbell, pest)!
Он негодяй (дурак, надоеда)!
awn n'i-guh-D'EYE (doo-RAHK, nuh-duh-YEH-duh)!

3

NUMERALS

CARDINAL

one один, одна, одно uh-D'EEN, uhd-NAH, uhd-NAW

two два, две, два dvah, dv'eh, dvah

three три tr'ee

four четыре chi-TY-r'eh

five пять p'aht'

six шесть shehst'

seven семь s'ehm'

eight восемь VAW-s'im'

nine девять D'EH-v'uht'

ten десять D'EH-s'uht'

eleven одиннадцать uh-D'EEN-nuh-tsuht'

twelve двенадцать dv'i-NAH-tsuht'

thirteen тринадцать tr'i-NAH-tsuht'

fourteen четырнадцать chi-TYR-nuh-tsuht'

fifteen пятнадцать p'uht-NAH-tsuht'

sixteen шестнадцать sh'yst-NAH-tsuht'

seventeen семнадцать s'im-NAH-tsuht'

eighteen восемнадцать vuh-s'im-NAH-tsuht'

nineteen девятнадцать d'i-v'uht-NAH-tsuht'

twenty двадцать DVAH-tsuht'

twenty-one двадцать один, одна, одно DVAH-tsuht' uh'-D'EEN (uhd-NAH, uhd-NAW)

twenty-two двадцать два, две, два DVAH-tsuht' dvah (dv'eh, dvah)

42

twenty-three двадцать три DVAH-tsuht' tr'ee

thirty тридцать TR'EE-tsuht'

forty сорок SAW-ruhk

fifty пятьдесят p'uht'-d'i-S'AHT

sixty шестьдесят shyst'-d'i-S'AHT

seventy семьдесят S'EHM'-d'i-s'uht

eighty восемьдесят VAW-s'im'-d'i-s'uht

ninety девяносто d'i-v'uh-NAWS-tuh

one hundred сто staw

two hundred двести DV'EHS-t'i

three hundred триста TR'EES-tuh

four hundred четыреста chi-TY-r'is-tuh

five hundred пятьсот p'uht'-SAWT

six hundred шестьсот shyst'-SAWT

seven hundred семьсот s'im'-SAWT

eight hundred восемьсот vuh-s'im'-SAWT

nine hundred девятьсот d'i-v'uht'-SAWT

one thousand тысяча TY-s'uh-chuh

five thousand пять тысяч p'aht' ty-S'AHCH

one million миллион m'il-l'i-AWN

one billion миллиард m'il-l'i-AHRT

ORDINAL

first первый P'EHR-vy

second второй ftuh-ROI

third третий TR'EH-t'ee

fourth четвёртый chit-V'AWR-ty

fifth пятый P'AH-ty

sixth шестой shys-TOI

seventh седьмой s'id'-MOI

43

eighth восьмой vuhs'-MOI

ninth девятый d'i-V'AH-ty

tenth десятый d'i-S'AH-ty

eleventh одиннадцатый uh-D'EEN-nuh-tsuh-ty

twelfth двенадцатый dv'eh-NAH-tsuh-ty

twentieth двадцатый dvuh-TSAH-ty

twenty-first двадцать первый DVAH-tsuht' P'EHR-vy

OTHERS

half a book пол книги pawl KN'EE-g'ee

half a page пол страницы pawl struh-N'EE-tsy

once однажды (*or* раз) uhd-NAHZH-dy (rahs)

twice дважды DVAHZH-dy

three times трижды TR'EEZH-dy

the first time первый раз P'EHR-vy rahs

the last time последний раз puhs-L'EHD-n'ee rahs

a dozen eggs дюжина яиц D'OO-zhy-nuh yuh-EETS

a pair of shoes пара ботинок PAH-ruh buh-T'EE-nuhk

44

4

TIME OF DAY, WEEK, MONTH, SEASONS, WEATHER, AGE

What day of the week is today?
Какой сегодня день недели?
kuh-KOI s'i-VAWD-n'uh d'ehn' n'i-D'EH-l'i?

Today is Monday.
Сегодня понедельник.
s'i-VAWD-n'uh puh-n'i-D'EHL'-n'ik.

Tuesday вторник FTAWR-n'ik	**Friday** пятница P'AHT-n'i-tsuh
Wednesday среда sr'i-DAH	**Saturday** суббота soob-BAW-tuh
Thursday четверг chit-V'EHRK	**Sunday** воскресенье vuh-skr'i-S'EH-n'eh

When were you here last?
Когда вы были здесь в последний раз?
kuhg-DAH vy BY-l'ee zd'ehs' fpuhs-L'EHD-n'ee rahs?

I was here in the month of January.
Я был (была) здесь в январе.
yah byl (by-LAH) zd'ehs' v'uhn-vuh-R'EH.

February в феврале f'i-vruh-L'EH

March в марте VMAHR-t'eh

April в апреле vuh-PR'EH-l'eh

May в мае VMAH-yeh

June в июне v'i-YOO-n'eh

What is today's date?
Какое сегодня число?
kuh-KAW-yeh s'i-VAWD-n'uh chis-LAW?

45

Today is the first (second, tenth) of July.
Сегодня первое (второе, десятое) июля.
s'VAWD-n'uh P'EHR-vuh-yeh (ftuh-RAW-yeh, d'i-S'AH-uh-yeh) ee-YOO-l'uh.

of August
августа
AHV-goos-tuh

of September
сентября
s'in-t'uh-BR'AH

of October
октября
uhk-t'uh-BR'AH

of November
ноября
nuh-yuh-BR'AH

of December
декабря
d'i-kuh-BR'AH

The spring (fall, winter) is beautiful.
Весна (осень, зима) прекрасна.
v'is-NAH (AW-s'in', z'i-MAH) pr'i-KRAHS-nuh.
yi.

The summer is beautiful.
Лето прекрасно на.
L'EH-tuh pr'i-KRAHS-nuh.

At what time do you wish to start?
В котором часу вы хотите двинуться?
fkuh-TAW-ruhm chuh-SOO vy khuh-T'EE-t'eh DV'EE-noot'-suh?

At (about) five (five-thirty) in the morning (afternoon).
В пять (около пяти) (в пять тридцать) утра (после полудня).
fp'aht' (AW-kuh-luh p'uh-T'EE) (fp'aht' TR'EE-tsuht') oo-TRAH (PAWS-l'eh puh-LOOD-n'uh).

At a quarter to eight in the evening.
Без четверти восемь вечера.
b'is CHEHT-v'ir-t'i VAW-s'im' V'EH-chi-ruh.

At eleven at night.
В одиннадцать ночи.
vuh-D'EEN-nuh-tsuht' NAW-chee.

At noon.
В полдень.
FPAWL-d'in'.

At midnight.
В полночь.
FPAWL-nuhch'.

At six at the latest.
Самое позднее в шесть.
SAH-muh-yeh PAWZ-dn'i-yeh fshehst'.

It's early (late).
Это рано (поздно).
EH-tuh RAH-nuh (PAWZ-dnuh).

What time is it?
Который час?
kuh-TAW-ry chahs?

It is two.
Два часа.
dvah chuh-SAH.

two-thirty.
два тридцать.
dvah TR'EE-tsuht'.

two-fifteen.
два пятнадцать,
dvah p'uht-NAH-tsuht'.

a quarter to three.
без четверти три.
b'is CHEHT-v'ir-t'i tr'ee.

ten minutes to three.
без десяти три.
b'iz d'i-s'uh-T'EE tr'ee.

ten minutes past three.
десять минут четвёртого.
D'EH-s'uht' m'i-NOOT chit-V'AWR-tuh-vuh.

47

I shall see him today.
Я увижу его сегодня.
yah oo-VEE-zhoo yi-VAW s'i-VAWD-n'uh.

tonight
сегодня вечером
s'i-VAWD-n'uh V'EH-chi-ruhm

this morning
сегодня утром
s'i-VAWD-n'uh OO-truhm

this afternoon
сегодня днём
s'i-VAWD-n'uh dn'awm

tomorrow
завтра
ZAHF-truh

day after tomorrow
послезавтра
puhs-l'i-ZAHF-truh

next year
в будущем году
VBOO-doosh-chim guh-DOO

next month
в следующем месяце
FSL'EH-doo-yoosh-chim M'EH-s'uh-tseh

next week
на следующей неделе
nuh SL'EH-doo-yoosh-chey n'i-D'EH-l'eh

We must start on time.
Мы должны отправиться во время.
my duhlzh-NY uht-PRAH-v'it'-suh VAW-vr'i-m'uh.

We must not be late.
Мы не должны опаздывать.
my n'i duhlzh-NY uh-PAHZ-dy-vuht'.

I saw him yesterday.
Я видел (видела) его вчера.
yah V'EE-d'il (V'EE-d'i-luh) yi-VAW fchi-RAH.

48

last night
вчера вечером
fchi-RAH V'EH-chi-ruhm

day before yesterday
позавчера
puh-zuhf-chi-RAH

last year
в прошлом году
FPRAWSH-luhm guh-DOO

last month
в прошлом месяце
FPRAWSH-luhm M'EH-s'uh-tseh

last week
на прошлой неделе
nuh PRAWSH-loi n'i-D'EH-l'eh

three days ago
три дня тому назад
tr'ee dn'ah tuh-MOO nuh-ZAHT

in a few days
через несколько дней
chi-r'iz-N'EH-skuhl'-kuh dn'ey

I see him every day (week, month).
Я вижу его каждый день (каждую неделю, каждый месяц).
yah V'EE-zhoo yi-VAW KAHZH-dy d'ehn' (KAHZH-doo-yoo
n'i-D'EH-l'oo, KAHZH-dy M'EH-s'uhts).

I stayed here all day.
Я провёл здесь весь день.
yah pruh-V'AWL zd'ehs v'ehs' d'ehn'.

all morning
всё утро
fs'aw OO-truh

all evening
весь вечер
v'ehs' V'EH-chir

all week
всю неделю
fs'oo n'i-D'EH-l'oo

the whole month
целый месяц
TSEH-ly M'EH-s'uhts

49

How old are you?
Сколько вам лет?
SKAWL'-kuh vahm l'eht?

I am twenty-five years old.
Мне двадцать пять лет.
mn'eh DVAH-tsuht' p'aht' l'eht.

How is the weather?
Какая погода?
kuh-KAH-yuh puh-GAW-duh?

It's fine weather.
Хорошая погода.
khuh-RAW-shuh-yuh puh-GAW-duh.

It's bad weather.
Плохая погода.
pluh-KHAH-yuh puh-GAW-duh.

It's warm.
Жарко.
ZHAHR-kuh.

It's cold.
Холодно.
KHAW-luhd-nuh.

It's windy.
Ветрено.
V'EH-tr'i-nuh.

It's sunny.
Солнечно.
SAWL-n'ich-nuh.

It is cloudy weather.
Облачная погода.
AW-bluhch-nuh-yuh puh-GAW-duh.

It's too hot (cold) to go today.
Сегодня слишком жарко (холодно) ехать.
s'i-VAWD-n'uh SL'EESH-kuhm ZHAHR-kuh (KHAW-luhd-nuh) YEH-khuht'.

I like the cold.
Я люблю холод.
yah l'oo-BL'OO KHAW-luht.

heat жару zhuh-ROO

sun солнце SAWN-ts'eh

fog туман too-MAHN

rain дождь dawzhd'

snow снег sn'ehk

hail град graht

wind ветер V'EH-t'ir

50

Do you feel cold?
Вам не холодно?
vahm n'i KHAW-luhd-nuh?

I feel warm.
Мне жарко.
mn'eh ZHAHR-kŭh.

It's starting to snow (rain).
Начал идти снег (дождь).
NAH-chuhl eet-T'EE sn'ehk (dawzhd').

It's beginning to clear up.
Начало проясняться.
NAH-chuh-luh pruh-yuh-SN'AHT'-suh.

It's snowing (raining).
Идёт снег (дождь).
ee-D'AWT sn'ehk (dawzhd').

It is hailing.
Идёт град.
ee-D'AWT graht.

It is thundering.
Гремит гром.
gr'i-M'EET grawm.

It is lightning.
Сверкает молния.
sv'ir-KAH-yit MAWL-n'i-yuh.

It's clearing up.
Проясняется.
pruh-yuh-SN'AH-yit-suh.

The sun (moon) is shining.
Солнце (луна) сияет.
SAWN-ts'eh (loo-NAH) s'i-YAH-yit.

The stars are out.
На небе звёзды.
nuh N'EH-b'eh ZV'AWZ-dy.

I am sleepy.
Чувствую себя сонным.
CHOOF-stvoo-yoo s'i-B'AH SAWN-nym.

It's cloudy.
Облачно.
AW-bluhch-nuh.

It's cool.
Прохладно.
pruh-KHLAHD-nuh.

It's foggy.
Туманно.
too-MAHN-nuh.

51

5

DIRECTIONS AND SIGNS

Where are you (we) going?
Куда вы идёте (мы идём)? *or* Куда вы едете (мы едем)?
koo-DAH vy ee-D'AW-t'eh (my ee-D'AWM)? koo-DAH vy
  YEH-d'i-t'eh (my YEH-d'im)?

Where is (are) ——?
Где ——?
gd'eh ——?

Here is (are) ——.
Тут ——.
toot ——.

Which way?
Каким путём?
kuh-K'EEM poo-T'AWM?

To the right (left).
Направо (налево).
nuh-PRAH-vuh (nuh-L'EH-vuh).

Straight ahead.
Прямо.
PR'AH-muh.

This (that) way.
Сюда (туда).
s'oo-DAH (too-DAH).

I'm looking for ——.
Я ищу ——.
yah yish-CHOO ——.

Can you tell me ——?
Можете ли вы сказать мне ——?
MAW-zhy-t'eh l'i vy skuh-ZAHT' mn'eh ——?

Please show me ——.
Пожалуйста покажите мне ——.
puh-ZHAL-stuh puh-kuh-ZHY-t'eh mn'eh ——.

52

No admittance.
Вход запрещается.
vkhawt zuh-pr'ish-CHAH-yit-suh.

No parking.
Запрещается ставить машину.
zuh-pr'ish-CHAH-yit-s'uh STAH-v'it' muh-SHY-noo.

No spitting.
Запрещается плевать.
zuh-pr'ish-CHAH-yit-suh pl'i-VAHT'.

Notice!
Оповещение!
uh-puh-v'ish-CHEH-n'i-yeh!

Keep right (left).
Держитесь правой (левой) стороны.
d'ir-ZHY-t'ehs' PRAH-voi (L'EH-voi) stuh-ruh-NY.

It is forbidden.
Это запрещается.
EH-tuh zuh-pr'ish-CHAH-yit-suh.

No smoking.
Курить воспрещается.
koo-R'EET' vuhs-pr'ish-CHAH-yit-suh.

Tourist Information Office.
Туристическое информационное бюро.
too-r'i-ST'EE-chis-kuh-yeh   yin-fuhr-muh-tsi-AWN-nuh-yeh
  b'oo-RAW.

Youth Hostel.
Общежитие для молодёжи.
uhbsh-chy-ZHY-t'i-yeh dl'uh muh-luh-D'AW-zhy.

Do not touch!
Не прикасайтесь!
n'i pr'i-kuh-SEYE-t'ehs'!

High-tension wires!
Ток высокого напряжения!
tawk vy-SAW-kuh-vuh nuh-pr'uh-ZHEH-n'i-yuh!

Crossroads.
Перекрёсток.
p'i-r'i-KR'AWS-tuhk.

53

Grade crossing.

Железная дорога.

zhy-L'EHZ-nuh-yuh duh-RAW-guh.

Watch out for trains!

Берегись поезда!

b'i-r'i-G'EES' PAW-yiz-duh!

Detour.

Обход (объезд).

uhb-KHAWT (uhb-YEHST).

Road closed (open).

Дорога закрыта (открыта).

duh-RAW-guh zuh-KRY-tuh (uht-KRY-tuh).

(Dangerous) curve!

(Опасная) кривая!

(uh-PAHS-nuh-yuh) kr'i-VAH-yuh!

Halt!	**Poison!**
Стой!	Яд!
stoi!	yaht!
Slow!	**Stop!**
Замедлите!	Остановитесь!
zuh-M'EHD-l'i-t'eh!	uh-stuh-nuh-V'EE-t'ehs'!

One way.

В одном направлении.

vuhd-NAWM nuh-pruhv-L'EH-n'ee-i.

No right (left) turn.

Не поворачивать направо (налево).

n'i puh-vuh-RAH-chy-vaht' nuh-PRAH-vuh (nuh-L'EH-vuh).

Pedestrians.

Пешеходы.

p'i-shy-KHAW-dy.

Do not lean out of windows.

Не высовываться из окна.

n'i vy-SAW-vy-vuht'-suh eez uhk-NAH.

Regular (signal) stop.

Нормальная (по сигналу) остановка.

nuhr-MAHL'-nuh-yuh (puh s'ig-NAH-loo) uhs-tuh-NAWF-
  kuh.

54

Full bus or streetcar (no more passengers).
Полон.
PAW-luhn.

Knock.
Постучите.
puh-stoo-CHEE-t'eh.

Entrance.
Вход.
vkhawt.

Ring the bell.
Звонок.
zvuh-NAWK.

Exit.
Выход.
VY-khuht.

Steep grade.
Крутой подъём.
kroo-TOI puhd-YAWM.

Road repairs.
Ремонт дороги.
r'i-MAWNT duh-RAW-g'ee.

School.
Школа.
SHKAW-luh.

No thoroughfare.
Нет проезда.
n'eht pruh-YEHZ-duh.

No trespassing.
Проход запрещается.
pruh-KHAWT zuh-pr'ish-CHAH-yit-suh.

Full stop.
Полная остановка.
PAWL-nuh-yuh uhs-tuh-NAWF-kuh.

Danger!
Опасность!
uh-PAHS-nuhst'!

Danger of death!
Смертельная опасность!
sm'ir-T'EHL'-nuh-yuh uh-PAHS-nuhst'!

Water not drinkable.
Вода не для питья.
vuh-DAH n'i dl'uh p'i-T'AH.

Do not cross the tracks.
Не переходите пути.
n'i p'i-r'i-khuh-D'EE-t'eh poo-T'EE.

Cashier.
Кассир.
kuhs-S'EER.

Ladies.
Дамская уборная.
DAHM-skuh-yuh oo-BAWR-nuh-yuh.

Gentlemen.
Мужская уборная.
moosh-SKAH-yuh oo-BAWR-nuh-yuh.

Free.
Свободно.
svuh-BAWD-nuh.

Occupied.
Занято.
ZAH-n'uh-tuh.

Wet paint.
Свеже покрашено.
SV'EH-zhy puh-KRAH-shy-nuh.

Keep off the grass.
Не ходить по траве.
n'i khuh-D'EET' puh truh-V'EH.

Quiet.
Тише.
T'EE-sheh.

Closed Sundays.
Закрыто по воскресеньям.
zuh-KRY-tuh puh vuhs-kr'i-S'EH-n'uhm.

Caution!
Осторожно!
uh-stuh-RAWZH-nuh!

Narrow bridge.
Узкий мост.
OOZ-k'ee mawst.

Speed limit fifty kilometers an hour.
Предельная скорость пятьдесят километров в час.
pr'i-D'EHL'-nuh-yuh SKAW-ruhst' p'uht'-d'i-S'AHT k'i-luh
    M'EH-truhf fchahs.

56

6

EMERGENCIES AND LANGUAGE DIFFICULTIES

Stop!
Стой!
stoi!

Stop that man!
Остановите этого человека!
uh-stuh-nuh-V'EE-t'eh EH-tuh-vuh chi-luh-V'EH-kuh!

Where did he go?
Куда он пошёл?
koo-DAH awn puh-SHAWL?

That way!
В эту сторону!
VEH-too STAW-ruh-noo!

Go away!
Уходите!
oo-khuh-D'EE-t'eh!

Get out!
Убирайтесь!
oo-b'i-REYE-t'ehs'!

Don't bother me!
Не беспокойте меня!
n'i b'is-puh-KOI-t'eh m'i-N'AH!

Look!
Смотрите!
smuh-TR'EE-t'eh!

Police!
Полиция!
puh-L'EE-tsi-yuh!

Call the police!
Позовите полицию!
puh-zuh-V'EE-t'eh puh-L'EE-tsi-yoo!

I've been robbed!
Меня обокрали!
m'i-N'AH uh-buh-KRAH-l'ee!

Where is the police station?
Где полицейский участок?
gd'eh puh-l'i-TSEY-sk'ee oo-CHAH-stuhk?

Fire!
Пожар!
puh-ZHAHR!

Help!
На помощь!
nuh PAW-muhshch'!

Come with me!
Идите со мной!
ee-D'EE-t'eh suh-MNOI!

I have lost ———.
Я потерял (потеряла) ———.
yah puh-t'i-R'AHL (puh-t'i-R'AH-luh) ———.

I can't find ———.
Я не могу найти ———.
yah n'i muh-GOO neye-T'EE ———.

Where did you leave it?
Где вы это оставили?
gd'eh vy EH-tuh uh-STAH-v'i-l'ee?

Where is the lost-and-found desk?
Где контора потерянных и найдённых вещей?
gd'eh kuhn-TAW-ruh puh-T'EH-r'uhn-nykh ee neye-D'AWN-
   nykh v'ish-CHEY?

What is happening?
Что происходит?
shtaw pruh-is-KHAW-d'it?

What's the matter?
В чём дело?
fchawm D'EH-luh?

What's the matter with you?
Что с вами случилось?
shtaw SVAH-m'ee sloo-CHEE-luhs'?

What do you want?
Что вы хотите?
shtaw vy khuh-T'EE-t'eh?

Who did it?
Кто это сделал?
ktaw EH-tuh SD'EH-luhl?

Don't worry!
Не беспокойтесь!
n'i b'is-puh-KOI-t'ehs'!

I don't remember.
Я не помню.
yah n'i PAWM-n'oo.

I forgot.
Я забыл (забыла).
yah zuh-BYL (zuh-BY-luh).

Can you ——?
Можете ли вы ——?
MAW-zhy-t'eh l'i vy ——?

What does that mean?
Что это значит?
shtaw EH-tuh ZNAH-chit?

I can't.
Я не могу.
yah n'i muh-GOO.

What do you mean?
Что вы хотите сказать?
shtaw vy khuh-T'EE-t'eh skuh-ZAHT'?

I've lost my way.
Я заблудился (заблудилась).
yah zuh-bloo-D'EEL-suh (zuh-bloo-D'EE-luhs').

I missed my train.
Я пропустил (пропустила) свой поезд.
yah pruh-poo-ST'EEL (pruh-poo-ST'EE-luh) svoi PAW-yist.

Do you know ——?
Вы знаете ——?
vy ZNAH-yi-t'eh ——?

Listen!
Слушайте!
SLOO-sheye-t'eh!

Help (direct) me!
Помогите мне (направьте меня)!
puh-muh-G'EE-t'eh mn'eh (nuh-PRAHV'-t'eh m'i-N'AH)!

Come here!
Идите сюда!
ee-D'EE-t'eh s'oo-DAH!

Hurry!
Поспешите!
puh-sp'i-SHY-t'eh!

What are you talking about?
О чём вы говорите?
uh CHAWM vy guh-vuh-R'EE-t'eh?

I don't know.
Я не знаю.
yah n'i ZNAH-yoo.

Do you understand?
Вы понимаете?
vy puh-n'i-MAH-yi-t'eh?

I don't understand.
Я не понимаю.
yah n'i puh-n'i-MAH-yoo

Look out!
Берегись! (*or* Берегитесь!)
b'i-r'i-G'EES'! (b'i-r'i-G'EE-t'ehs'l)

One moment!
Сию минуту!
s'i-YOO m'i-NOO-tool

Do you speak English?
Вы говорите по-английски?
vy guh-vuh-R'EE-t'eh puh-uhn-GL'EE-sk'ee?

I don't speak Russian.
Я не говорю по-русски.
yah n'i guh-vuh-R'OO puh-ROOS-k'ee.

A little.
Немного.
n'im-NAW-guh.

Speak more slowly.
Говорите медленнее.
guh-vuh-R'EE-t'eh M'EHD-l'i-n'i-yeh.

Please repeat.
Повторите пожалуйста.
puhf-tuh-R'EE-t'eh puh-ZHAHL-stuh.

What do you call this in Russian?
Как это называется по-русски?
kahk EH-tuh nuh-zy-VAH-yit-suh puh-ROOS-k'ee?

I have left my coat on the bus.
Я оставил (оставила) пальто в автобусе.
yah uh-STAH-v'il (uh-STAH-v'i-luh) puhl'-TAW vuhf-TAW
boo-s'eh.

on the plane
в аэроплане (*or* в самолёте)
vuh-eh-ruh-PLAH-n'eh (fsuh-muh-L'AW-t'eh)

on the train
в поезде
FPAW-yiz-d'eh

on the ship
на пароходе
nuh puh-ruh-KHAW-d'eh

How can I recover it?
Как я могу получить это обратно?
kahk yah muh-GOO puh-loo-CHEET' EH-tuh uh-BRAHT-
nuh?

Please forward it to me at Moscow.
Перешлите это мне пожалуйста в Москву.
p'i-r'i-SHL'EE-t'eh EH-tuh mn'eh puh-ZHAHL-stuh vmuhsk-
VOO.

I am an American.
Я американец (американка).
yah uh-m'i-r'i-KAH-n'ehts (uh-m'i-r'i-KAHN-kuh).

Take me to the American Consul.
Отвезите меня к американскому консулу.
uht-v'i-Z'EE-t'eh m'i-N'AH kuh-m'i-r'i-KAHN-skuh-moo
KAWN-soo-loo.

Where is the lavatory?
Где уборная?
gd'eh oo-BAWR-nuh-yuh?

Upstairs and to the right.
Наверху направо.
nuh-v'ir-KHOO nuh-PRAH-vuh.

How do you say —— in Russian?
Как сказать —— по-русски?
kahk skuh-ZAHT' —— puh-ROOS-k'ee?

7
PLACES OF INTEREST (CHURCHES, THEATERS, SIGHTSEEING, NIGHT LIFE)

Do you need a guide?
Нужен ли вам гид?
NOO-zhyn l'ee vahm G'EET?

Is the museum open now (on Sunday)?
Открыт ли сейчас музей (в воскресенье)?
uht-KRYT l'i s'ey-CHAHS moo-Z'EY (vuh-skr'i-S'EH-n'yeh)?

It is closed on Monday.
По понедельникам он закрыт.
puh puh-n'i-D'EHL'-n'i-kuhm awn zuh-KRYT.

Is admission free?
Вход свободный?
FKHAWT svuh-BAWD-ny?

Admission is five rubles.
За вход пять рублей.
zuh fkhawt p'aht' roo-BL'EY.

Is it permitted to take photographs?
Разрешается ли фотографировать?
ruhz-r'i-SHAH-yit-suh l'i fuh-tuh-gruh-F'EE-ruh-vuht'?

It is forbidden; but we sell souvenir post cards.
Это запрещено; но мы продаём открытки на память.
EH-tuh zuh-pr'ish-chi-NAW; nuh my pruh-duh-YAWM uht-KRYT-k'ee nuh PAH-m'uht'.

What are the places of interest here?
Какие достопримечательности имеются здесь?
kuh-K'EE-yeh   duh-stuh-pr'i-m'i-CHAH-t'il'-nuh-st'i   ee-M'EH-yoot-suh zd'ehs'?

Where is the cathedral (church, synagogue, monastery)?
Где собор (церковь, синагога, монастырь)?
gd'eh suh-BAWR (TS'ER-kuhv', s'i-nuh-GAW-guh, muh-nuh-STYR')?

    the university университет oo-n'i-v'ir-s'i-T'EHT

the **fountain** фонтан fuhn-TAHN

the **garden** сад saht

the **park** парк pahrk

the **square** площадь PLAWSH-chuht'

the **bridge** мост mawst

the **imperial palace** царский дворец TSAHR-sk'ee dvuh-R'EHTS

the **opera house** опера AW-p'i-ruh

the **museum** музей moo-Z'EY

the **gallery** галлерея guhl-l'i-R'EH-yuh

the **monument** памятник PAH-m'uht-n'ik

the **harbor** гавань GAH-vuhn', *or* порт pawrt

the **river** река r'i-KAH

What time is (high) Mass (service in English)?
В какое время (главная) церковная служба (на английском языке)?
fkuh-KAW-yeh VR'EH-m'uh (GLAHV-nuh-yuh) ts'ir-KAWV-nuh-yuh SLOOZH-buh (nuh uhn-GL'EE-skuhm yuh-zy-K'EH)?

I want to see a priest (minister, rabbi).
Я хотел (хотела) бы видеть священника (пастора, раввина).
yah khuh-T'EHL (khuh-T'EH-luh) by V'EE-d'cht' sv'uhsh-CHEHN-n'i-kuh (PAH-stuh-ruh, ruhv-V'EE-nuh).

Where is the entrance (exit)?
Где вход (выход)?
gd'eh vkhawt (VY-khawt)?

Where are the theaters?
Где находятся театры?
gd'eh nuh-KHAW-d'it-suh t'i-AH-try?

Is this the box office?
Это театральная касса?
EH-tuh t'i-uh-TRAHL'-nuh-yuh KAHS-suh?

At what time does the performance start?
В котором часу начало представления?
fkuh-TAW-ruhm chuh-SOO nuh-CHAH-luh pr'id-stuh-VL'EH-n'i-yuh?

At what time is it over?
Когда оно кончается?
kuhg-DAH uh-NAW kuhn-CHAH-yit-suh?

May I see your ticket?
Можно посмотреть ваш билет?
MAWZH-nuh puh-smuh-TR'EHT' vahsh b'i-L'EHT?

There is a concert this evening at eight-thirty.
Концерт сегодня вечером в восемь тридцать.
kuhn-TSEHRT s'i-VAWD-n'uh V'EH-chi-ruhm VAW-s'im
TR'EE-tsuht'.

> **a festival** фестивал f'is-t'i-VAHL

> **a ball (dance)** бал bahl

> **a performance** представление pr'id-stuh-VL'EH-n'i-
> yeh

> **a motion picture** кинематограф k'i-n'i-muh-TAW-
> gruhf

Where can we go to dance?
Куда мы можем пойти танцовать?
koo-DAH my MAW-zhym poi-T'EE tuhn-tsuh-VAHT'?

A table for two, please.
Стол для двоих пожалуйста.
stawl dl'uh dvuh-EEKH puh-ZHAHL-stuh.

The cover charge is five rubles.
За место следует пять рублей.
zuh M'EHS-tuh SL'EH-doo-yit p'aht' roo-BL'EY.

Are evening clothes necessary?
Обязательно ли быть в вечернем платье?
uh-b'uh-ZAH-t'il'-nuh l'i byt' v'i-CHEHR-n'im PLAH-t'eh?

The menu (wine list, bill), please.
Меню (прейс-курант вин, счёт), пожалуйста.
m'i-N'OO (pr'eys-koo-RAHNT V'EEN, schawt), puh-ZHAHL-
stuh.

Ask the orchestra to play "Ochi chorniye."
Попросите оркестр сыграть "Очи Чёрные."
puh-pruh-S'EE-t'ch uhr-K'EHSTR sy-GRAHT' AW-chee
CHAWR-ny-yeh

Are you the usher?

Вы местоуказатель (местоуказательница)?

vy m'is-tuh-oo-kuh-ZAH-t'il' (m'is-tuh-oo-kuh-ZAH-t'il'-n'i-tsuh)?

What opera (play, comedy, film) is playing tonight?

Какая опера (пьеса, комедия, какой фильм) идёт сегодня?

kuh-KAH-yuh AW-p'i-ruh (P'EH-suh, kuh-M'EH-d'i-yuh, kuh-KOI feel'm) ee-D'AWT s'i-VAWD-nyuh)?

Please give me a balcony seat (box, orchestra) for Wednesday afternoon.

Дайте пожалуйста место на балконе (в ложе, в партере) на среду после полудня.

DEYE-t'eh puh-ZHAHL-stuh M'EHS-tuh nuh buhl-KAW-n'eh (VLAW-zheh, fpuhr-T'EH-r'eh) nuh sr'i-DOO PAWS-l'eh puh-LOOD-n'uh.

Here is a seat in the third row.

Тут есть место в третьем ряду.

toot yehst' M'EH-stuh FTR'EH-t'im r'uh-DOO.

Do we have to stand in line?

Станем в очередь?

STAH-n'im VAW-chi-r'id'?

May I buy a program?

Можно купить программу?

MAWZH-nuh koo-PEET' pruh-GRAHM-moo?

Where is the checkroom?

Где раздевальная?

gd'eh ruhz-d'i-VAHL'-nuh-yuh?

I should like to visit a night club.

Я хотел (хотела) бы посетить ночной ресторан.

yah khuh-T'EHL (khuh-T'EH-luh) by puh-s'i-T'EET' nuhch-NOI r'is-tuh-RAHN.

8

MONEY, BANK, MEASURES

Where is the bank?
Где банк?
gd'eh BAHNK?

I have no money (change).
У меня нет денег (мелочи).
oo m'i-N'AH n'eht D'EH-n'ehk (M'EH-luh-chee).

Can you change a $20 bill?
Можете ли вы разменять двадцать долларов?
MAW-zhy-t'eh l'i vy ruhz-m'i-N'AHT' DVAH-tsuht' DAWL-luh-ruhf?

Can you cash an international (telegraphic) money order?
Можете ли вы разменять международный (телеграфный) денежный перевод?
MAW-zhy-t'eh l'i vy ruhz-m'i-N'AHT' m'izh-doo-nuh-RAWD-ny (t'i-l'i-GRAHF-ny) D'EH-n'izh-ny p'i-r'i-VAWT?

Let me have some small change.
Дайте мне немного мелочи.
DEYE-t'eh mn'eh n'im-NAW-guh M'EH-luh-chee.

Can you cash a check?
Можете ли вы кассировать чек?
MAW-zhy-t'eh l'i vy kuhs-S'EE-ruh-vuht' chehk?

We cannot take a personal check.
Мы не можем брать личных чеков.
my n'eh MAW-zhym braht' L'EECH-nykh CHEH-kuhf.

Is this check made out to you?
Этот чек выписан на ваше имя?
EH-tuht chehk VY-p'i-suhn nuh VAH-sheh EE-m'uh?

Please endorse it (sign here).
Пожалуйста подпишите на обороте (подпишите здесь).
uh-ZHAHL-stuh puht-p'i-SHY-t'eh nuh uh-buh-RAW-t'eh (puht-p'i-SHY-t'eh zd'ehs').

What is the (best) rate today?
Какой (наилучший) курс сегодня?
kuh-KOI (neye-LOOCH-shy) koors s'i-VAWD-n'uh?

Four rubles to the dollar.
Четыре рубля за доллар.
chi-TY-r'eh roo-BL'AH zuh DAWL-luhr.

Where can I change dollars?
Где я могу обменять доллары?
gd'eh yah muh-GOO uhb-m'i-N'AHT' DAWL-luh-ry?

At the bank (hotel, exchange office).
В банке (в отеле, в меняльной конторе).
VBAHN-k'eh (vuh-T'EH-l'eh, vm'i-N'AHL'-noi kuhn-TAW-r'eh).

At what time does the bank open?
В котором часу открывается банк?
fkuh-TAW-ruhm chuh-SOO uht-kry-VAH-yit-suh bahnk?

It opens at 10 and stays open till 3.
Он открывается в десять и открыт до трёх.
awn uht-kry-VAH-yit-suh VD'EH-s'uht' ee uht-KRYT duh tr'awkh.

Can I borrow money at the bank?
Могу ли я занять денег в банке?
muh-GOO l'i yah zuh-N'AHT' D'EH-n'ehk VBAHN-k'eh?

Perhaps they will lend you some money.
Может быть они смогут одолжить вам деньги.
MAW-zhyt byt' uh-N'EE SMAW-goot uh-duhl-ZHYT' vahm D'EHN'-g'ee.

Do you accept traveler's checks?
Принимаете ли вы путевые чеки?
pr'i-n'i-MEYE-t'eh l'i vy poo-t'i-VY-yeh CHEH-k'ee?

We (do not) accept them.
Мы (не) принимаем их.
my (n'ch) pr'i-n'i-MAH-yim eekh.

I should like to change this (make out a draft).
Я хотел (хотела) бы это разменять (сделать перевод).
yah khuh-T'EHL (khuh-T'EH-luh) by EH-tuh ruhz-m'i-N'AHT' (ZD'EH-luht' p'i-r'i-VAWT).

May I speak to the manager?

Могу ли я поговорить с управляющим?

muh-GOO l'i yah puh-guh-vuh-R'EET' soo-pruh-VL'AH-
yoosh-chim?

He's busy right now; will you wait?

Он сейчас как раз занят; хотите его подождать?

awn s'ey-CHAHS kahk rahz ZAH-n'uht; khuh-T'EE-t'eh yi-
VAW puh-duhzh-DAHT'?

MEASURES

meter (39.37 inches, or 3.38 feet, or 1.09 yards)
метр
m'ehtr

centimeter (0.39 inches)
сантиметр
suhn-t'i-M'EHTR

kilometer (0.621 miles)
километр
k'i-luh-M'EHTR

liter (1.75 pints)
литр
l'eetr

gram (0.0352 ounces)
грамм
grahm

hectogram (3.52 ounces)
гектограмм
g'ik-tuh-GRAHM

kilogram (2.20 pounds)
килограмм
k'i-luh-GRAHM

9

WRITING AND POST OFFICE

Where is the mailbox?
Где почтовый ящик?
gd'eh puhch-TAW-vy YAHSH-chik?

the stamp window
продажа марок
pruh-DAH-zhuh MAH-ruhk

Where is the registry window?
Где сдаются заказные письма?
gd'eh sduh-YOO-tsuh zuh-kuhz-NY-yeh P'EES'-muh?

Where is the parcel-post window?
Где отделение для посылок?
gd'eh uht-d'i-L'EH-n'i-yeh dl'uh puh-SY-luhk?

Where is the money-order window?
Где отделение для денежных переводов?
gd'eh uht-d'eh uht-d'i-L'EH-n'i-yeh dl'uh D'EH-n'izh-nykh p'i-r'i-VAW-duhf?

How much is an insured (registered, special-delivery) letter to Moscow?
Сколько стоит застрахованное (заказное, срочное) письмо в Москву?
SKAWL'-kuh STAW-yit zuh-struh-KHAW-vuhn-nuh-yeh (zuh-kuhz-NAW-yeh, SRAWCH-nuh-yeh) p'is'-MAW vmuhs-KVOO?

I want to send this parcel insured.
Я хочу послать этот пакет застрахованным.
yah khuh-CHOO puhs-LAHT' EH-tuht puh-K'EHT zuhs-truh-KHAW-vuhn-nym.

The regular (air-mail) rate is fifty kopeks per gram.
Тариф за обычное письмо (за письмо воздушной почтой) пятьдесят копеек за грамм.
tuh-R'EEF zuh uh-BYCH-nuh-yeh p'is'-MAW (zuh p'is'-MAW vuhz-DOOSH-noi PAWCH-toi) p'uht'-d'i-S'AHT kuh-P'EH-yik zuh grahm.

69

I want a pen (ink, writing paper).

Я хотел (хотела) бы перо (чернила, писчей бумаги).

yah khuh-T'EHL (khuh-T'EH-luh) by p'i-RAW (chir-N'EE-luh, P'EES-chey boo-MAH-g'ee).

I want to write a letter (send a post card).

Я хочу написать письмо (послать открытку).

yah khuh-CHOO nuh-p'i-SAHT' p'is'-MAW (puhs-LAHT' uht-KRYT-koo).

Please mail this letter for me.

Пошлите пожалуйста это письмо.

puhsh-L'EE-t'eh puh-ZHAHL-stuh EH-tuh p'is'-MAW.

Have you any letters for me?

Есть ли у вас письма для меня?

YEHST'-l'i oo vahs P'EES'-muh dl'uh m'i-N'AH?

Give me five stamps.

Дайте мне пять марок.

DEYE-t'eh mn'eh p'aht' MAH-ruhk.

ten post cards	eight envelopes
десять открыток	восемь конвертов
D'EH-~'uht' uht-KRY-tuhk	VAW-s'im' kuhn-V'EHR-tuhf
Sender.	**Receiver.**
Отправитель.	Получатель.
uht-prn -V'EE-t'ehl'.	puh-loo-CHAH-t'ehl'.

Where is the general-delivery window?

Где окошко до востребования?

gd'eh uh-KAWSH-kuh duh vuhs-TR'EH-buh-vuh-n'i-yuh?

Where is the post office?

Где почтовое отделение (or почтовая контора)?

gd'eh puhch-TAW-vuh-yeh uht-d'i-L'EH-n'i-yeh (puhch-TAW-vuh-yuh kuhn-TAW-ruh)?

When is it open?

Когда оно открыто (or она открыта)?

kuhg-DAH uh-NAW uht-KRY-tuh (uh-NAH uht-KRY-tuh)?

What is the regular (air-mail) postage to New York?

Сколько стоит обычное (воздушной почтой) письмо в Нью-Йорк?

SKAWL'-kuh STAW-yit uh-BYCH-nuh-yeh (vuhz-DOOSH-noi PAWCH-toi) p'is'-MAW vn'oo-YAWRK?

10

How many are you?

Сколько вас?

SKAWL'-kuh vahs?

A table for two, please, near the window.

Пожалуйста столик для двоих возле окна.

puh-ZHAHL-stuh STAW-l'ik dl'uh dvuh-EEKH VAWZ-l'i
uhk-NAH.

This table is reserved.

Этот стол занят.

EH-tuht stawl ZAH-n'uht.

This way, sir.

Сюда пожалуйста, гражданин.

s'oo-DAH puh-ZHAHL-stuh, gruhzh-duh-N'EEN.

Do you want a cocktail?

Желаете коктэйль?

zhy-LEYE-t'eh kuhk-TEYL'?

Give us an apéritif (whiskey, gin, a liqueur).

Дайте нам аперитив (виски, джин, ликёр).

DEYE-t'eh nahm uh-p'i-r'i-T'EEF (V'EES-k'ee, djeen, l'i-
K'AWR).

Have you a table d'hôte dinner (breakfast, lunch)?

Есть ли у вас табль-дот обед (утренний чай, завтрак)?

YEHST'-l'i oo vahs tahbl'-DAWT uh-B'EHT (OO-tr'in-n'i
cheye, ZAHF-truhk)?

**Yes sir; for ten rubles we give you appetizers, soup, a
meat course with two vegetables, salad and dessert.**

Да; за десять рублей даётся закуска, суп, жаркое с зеленью,
салат и дессерт.

dah; zuh D'EH-s'uht' roo-BL'EY duh-YAWT-suh zuh-
KOOS-kuh, soop, zhuhr-KAW-yeh SZ'EH-l'i-n'oo, suh-
LAHT ee d'is-S'EHRT.

Let me have the menu (wine list).

Дайте мне меню (прейскурант вин).

DEYE-t'eh mn'eh m'i-N'OO (pr'eys-koo-RAHNT v'een).

What is today's special?

Какое сегодня специальное блюдо?

kuh-KAW-yeh s'i-VAWD-n'uh sp'i-tsi-AHL'-nuh-yeh BL'OO-duh?

What wine (dish) do you recommend?

Какое вино (блюдо) вы рекомендуете?

kuh-KAW-yeh v'i-NAW (BL'OO-duh) vy r'i-kuh-m'in-DOO-yi-t'eh?

I'm hungry and thirsty.

Я голоден (голодна) и хочу пить.

yah GAW-luh-d'in (guh-luhd-NAH) ee khuh-CHOO p'eet'.

What would you like to eat and drink?

Что бы вы хотели съесть и выпить?

shtaw by vy khuh-T'EH-l'i syehst' ee VY-p'it'?

Where can we find a good restaurant?

Где мы можем найти хороший ресторан?

gd'eh my MAW-zhym neye-T'EE khuh-RAW-shy r'is-tuh-RAHN?

Here's one.

Вот один.

vawt uh-D'EEN.

, you prefer baked, boiled, broiled or stewed meat?

едпочитаете ли вы печёное, варёное, жареное или тушёное
мясо?

'id-puh-chi-TEYE-t'eh l'i vy p'i-CHAW-nuh-yeh, vuh-R'AW-nuh-yeh, ZHAH-r'i-nuh-yeh EE-l'ee too-SHAW-nuh-yeh M'AH-suh?

'ike the steak well done (medium, rare).

люблю бифштекс хорошо прожаренный (средне прожарен-ный, кровавый).

,uh l'oo-BL'OO b'if-SHTEHKS khuh-ruh-SHAW pruh-ZHAH-r'in-ny (SR'ED-n'eh pruh-ZHAH-r'in-ny, kruh-VAH-vy).

ring me another portion.

'ринесите мне ещё одну порцию.

'i-n'i-S'EE-t'eh mn'eh yish-CHAW uhd-NOO PAWR-tsi-yoo.

at does the hors d'oeuvre consist of?

) даётся на закуску?

'aw duh-YAWT-suh nuh zuh-KOOS-koo?

old cuts холодное мясо khu-LAWD-nuh-yeh M'AH-suh

salami салями suh-L'AH-m'ee

sardines сардинки suhr-D'EEN-k'ee

hard-boiled eggs крутые яйца kroo-TY-yeh YEYE-tsuh

cucumbers огурцы uh-goor-TSY

peppers зелёный перец z'i-L'AW-ny P'EH-r'its

We should like to have a Russian-style dinner.
Мы хотели бы получить настоящий русский обед.
my khuh-T'EH-l'i by puh-loo-CHEET' nuh-stuh-YAHSH-chy ROOS-k'ee uh-B'EHT.

breakfast утренний чай OO-tr'in-n'i cheye

lunch завтрак ZAHF-truhk

supper ужин OO-zhyn

Bring us two orders of soup.
Принесите нам две порции супа.
pr'i-n'i-S'EE-t'eh nahm dv'eh PAWR-tsi-yi SOO-puh.

goose гуся GOO-s'uh

chicken циплёнка tsi-PL'AWN-kuh

ham ветчины v'it-chi-NY

eggs яйца YEYE-tsuh

omelet яичницу yuh-EECH-n'i-tsoo

liver печёнку p'i-CHAWN-koo

sausage колбасы kuhl-buh-SY

shrimps креветок kr'i-V'EH-tuhk

lobster лангустов luhn-GOOS-tuhf

of oysters устриц OO-str'its

of fish рыбы RY-by

roast beef ростбиф RAWST-b'if

lamb баранину buh-RAH-n'i-noo

duck утку OOT-koo

73

Do you want fried, boiled or mashed potatoes?
Желаете вы картофель жареный, варёный или пюре?
zhy-LEYE-t'eh vy kuhr-TAW-f'il' ZHAH-r'i-ny, vuh-R'AY
ny EE-l'ee p'oo-R'EH?

I'd rather have rice.
Я предпочёл бы рис.
yah pr'id-puh-CHAWL by r'ees.

**Shall I make you a salad with lettuce, celery, tomatoe
olives, radishes and onions?**
Сделать вам салат из латука, сельдерея, помидор, оливко
редиски и лука?
SD'EH-luht' vahm suh-LAHT eez luh-TOO-kuh, s'il'-d
R'EH-yuh, puh-m'i-DAWR, uh-L'EEF-kuhf, r'i-D'EES-k
ee LOO-kuh?

What kind of chops do you have?
Какие у вас отбивные котлеты?
kuh-K'EE-yeh oo vahs uht-b'iv-NY-yeh kuht-L'EH-ty?

Lamb, pork and veal.
Баранина, свинина и телятина.
buh-RAH-n'i-nuh, sv'i-N'EE-nuh ee t'i-L'AH-t'i-nuh.

What have you for dessert?
Что у вас на дессерт?
shtaw oo vahs nuh d'is-S'EHRT?

**Cheese and fruit, ice cream, pastry, pie, pudding and
cake.**
Сыр и фрукты, мороженое, пирожные, пирог, пуддинг и
кэкс.
syr ee FROOK-ty, muh-RAW-zhy-nuh-yeh, p'i-RAWZH-ny-
yeh, p'i-RAWK, POOD-d'ink ee kehks.

What vegetables do you have?
Какие у вас овощи?
kuh-K'EE-yeh oo vahs AW-vuhsh-chee?

beans бобы buh-BY

peas горошек guh-RAW-shik

carrots морковь muhr-KAWF'

string beans зелёные бобы z'i-L'AW-ny-yeh buh-BY

artichokes артишоки uhr-t'i-SHAW-k'ee

spinach шпинат shp'i-NAHT

mushrooms грибы gr'i-BY

cabbage капуста kuh-POOS-tuh

cauliflower цветная капуста tsv'it-NAH-yuh kuh-PO tuh

beets свёкла SV'AW-kluh

asparagus спаржа SPAHR-zhuh

Please bring oil and vinegar.
Дайте пожалуйста прованское масло и уксус.
DEYE-t'eh puh-ZHAHL-stuh pruh-VAHN-skuh-yeh MAHS-luh ee OOK-soos.

salt and pepper
соль и перец
sawl' ee P'EH-r'its

bread and butter
хлеб и масло
khl'ehp ee MAHS-luh

some rolls
булочки
BOO-luhch-k'ee

sugar and lemon
сахар и лимон
SAH-khuhr ee l'i-MAWN

a napkin
салфетку
suhl-F'EHT-koo

another plate
другую тарелку
droo-GOO-yoo tuh-R'EHL-koo

a soup dish
глубокую тарелку
gloo-BAW-koo-yoo tuh-R'EHL-koo

ice water
воды со льдом
vuh-DY suh l'dawm

ice
льду
l'doo

75

milk and cream
молоко и сливки
muh-luh-KAW ee SL'EEF-k'ee

a knife and fork
нож и вилку
nawsh ee V'EEL-koo

a spoon and a teaspoon
столовую ложку и чайную ложку
stuh-LAW-voo-yoo LAWSH-koo **ee** CHEYE-noo-yoo
LAWSH-koo

a water glass (a wine glass)
стакан (рюмку)
stuh-KAHN (R'OOM-koo)

a cup and a saucer
чашку и блюдечко
CHAHSH-koo ee BL'OO-d'ich-kuh

Let me have some more sauce.
Дайте мне ещё соуса.
DEYE-t'eh mn'eh yish-CHAW SAW-oo-suh.

I should like a cup of tea (black coffee, coffee with milk).
Я хотел (хотела) бы стакан чаю (чёрного кофе, кофе с
молоком).
yah khuh-T'EHL (khuh-T'EH-luh) by stuh-KAHN CHAH-yoo
(CHAWR-nuh-vuh KAW-f'eh, KAW-f'eh smuh-luh-
KAWM).

Let me have a glass (bottle) of beer.
Дайте мне стакан (бутылку) пива.
DEYE-t'eh mn'eh stuh-KAHN (boo-TYL-koo) P'EE-vuh.

of white wine белого вина B'EH-luh-vuh v'i-NAH

of red wine красного вина KRAHS-nuh-vuh v'i-NAH

of sparkling wine шипучего вина shy-POO-chi-vuh v'i-
NAH

of mineral water минеральной воды m'i-n'i-RAHL'-
noi vuh-DY

of vodka водки VAWT-k'ee

This meat is cold (tough, overdone, not cooked enough).
Это мясо холодное (твёрдое, переварено, недожарено).
EH-tuh M'AH-suh khuh-LAWD-nuh-yeh (TV'AWR-duh-yeh,
p'i-r'i-VAH-r'i-nuh, n'i-duh-ZHAH-r'i-nuh).

I should like to have for breakfast orange juice or prunes.

Я хотел (хотела) бы к утреннему чаю апельсинный сок или сливы.

yah khuh-T'EHL (khuh-T'EH-luh) by KOO-tr'in-n'i-moo CHAH-yoo uh-p'il'-S'EEN-ny sawk EE-l'ee SL'EE-vy.

bacon and eggs

поджареное сало и яйца

puhd-ZHAH-r'i-nuh-yeh SAH-luh ee YEYE-tsuh

ham and eggs

ветчину с яйцами

v'it-chi-NOO S'EYE-tsuh-m'ee

toast and jam

поджареный хлеб и варенье

puhd-ZHAH-r'i-ny khl'ehp ee vuh-R'EH-n'eh

Please call the waiter (waitress, headwaiter).

Позовите пожалуйста слугу (подавальщицу, метр д'отеля).

puh-zuh-V'EE-t'eh puh-ZHAHI -stuh sloo-GOO (puh-duh-VAHL'SH-chi-tsoo, m'ehtr duh-T'EH-l'uh).

This fork is not clean.

Эта вилка не чистая.

EH-tuh V'EEL-kuh n'i CHEES-tuh-yuh.

This table cloth is not clean.

Эта скатерть грязная.

EH-tuh SKAH-t'irt' GR'AHZ-nuh-yuh.

What would you like to drink?

Что желаете пить?

shtaw zhy-LEYE-t'eh p'eet'?

Please change it.

Перемените её пожалуйста.

p'i-r'i-m'i-N'EE-t'ch yi-YAW puh-ZHAHL-stuh.

I did not order this.

Я этого не заказывал (заказывала).

yah EH-tuh-vuh n'i zuh-KAH-zy-vuhl (zuh-KAH-zy-vuh-luh).

May I change my order?

Могу ли я переменить заказ?

muh-GOO l'i yah p'i-r'i-m'i-N'EET' zuh-KAHS?

This is too sweet.
Это слишком сладко.
EH-tuh SL'EESH-kuhm SLAHT-kuh.

sour кисло K'EES-luh

bitter горько GAWR'-kuh

salty солоно SAW-luh-nuh

not well seasoned не хорошо приправлено n'i khuh-ruh-SHAW pr'i-PRAHV-l'i-nuh

not tasty не вкусно n'i FKOOS-nuh

Bring the coffee now.
Принесите теперь кофе.
pr'i-n'i-S'EE-t'eh t'i-P'EHR' KAW-f'eh.

More coffee (water), please.
Пожалуйста ещё кофе (воды).
puh-ZHAHL-stuh yish-CHAW KAW-f'eh (vuh-DY).

At once, sir.
Сейчас.
s'ey-CHAHS.

What fruit have you?
Какие есть у вас фрукты?
kuh-K'EE-yeh yehst' oo vahs FROOK-ty?

cherries вишни V'EESH-n'ee

grapes виноград v'i-nuh-GRAHT

strawberries клубника kloob-N'EE-kuh

tangerines мандарины muhn-duh-R'EE-ny

nuts орехи uh-R'EH-khee

bananas бананы buh-NAH-ny

pineapple ананас uh-nuh-NAHS

figs фиги F'EE-g'ee

almonds миндаль m'in-DAHL'

hazelnuts обыкновенные орехи uh-byk-nuh-V'EHN-ny-yeh uh-R'EH-khee

78

peaches персики P'EHR-s'i-k'ee

plums сливы SL'EE-vy

apples яблоки YAH-bluh-k'ee

melon дыня DY-n'uh

watermelon арбуз uhr-BOOS

pears груши GROO-shy

apricots абрикосы uh-br'i-KAW-sy

oranges апельсины uh-p'il'-S'EE-ny

There's a mistake in the bill.
Тут в счёте ошибка.
toot FSCHAW-t'eh uh-SHEEP-kuh.

Please pay the cashier.
Пожалуйста заплатите кассиру.
puh-ZHAHL-stuh zuh-pluh-T'EE-t'ch kuhs-S'EE-roo.

The check, please.
Дайте пожалуйста счёт.
DEYE-t'eh puh-ZHAHL-stuh schawt.

Is the service included?
Услуги включены в счёт?
oo-SLOO-g'ee fkl'oo-chi-NY fschawt?

This is for you.
Это для вас.
EH-tuh dl'uh vahs.

Keep the change.
Оставьте себе сдачу.
uhs-TAHF'-t'eh s'i-B'EH SDAH-choo.

баклажан (buh-kluh-ZHAHN) Eggplant, aubergine.

маринованные баклажаны (muh-r'i-NAW-vuhn-ny-yeh buh-kluh-ZHAH-ny) Eggplant pickled with carrots, garlic and celery.

чебуреки (chi-boo-R'EH-k'ee) Thin, crisp, somewhat tough pastry stuffed with ground beef or lamb, chopped onions and spices, then fried in deep fat. A specialty of the Caucasian and Ukrainian Cossacks.

шампиньоны (shuhm-p'i-N'AW-ny) White mushrooms (*champignons*).

шашлык (shuhsh-LYK) Slices of mutton roasted on skewers.

кавказский шашлык (kuhf-KAHS-k'ee shuhsh-LYK) Pieces of loin or leg of mutton roasted on a skewer with alternate slices of onion and tomato. Served with plain boiled rice. A specialty of the Caucasus.

шпроты (SHPRAW-ty) Small sardines smoked golden brown and served in olive oil.

щи (shchee) A soup made with beef stock, cabbage, onions, flour, fennel, and served with sour cream.

кислые щи (K'EES-ly-yeh shchee) A soup made with beef stock, braised sauerkraut, lean bacon, tomatoes, chopped parsley and sour cream.

крапивные щи (kruh-P'EEV-ny-yeh shchee) A soup made with blanched nettles, sorrel and sausages, and served with sour cream.

(фаршированная) щука по польски (fuhr-shy-RAW-vuhn-nuh-yuh SHCHOO-kuh puh-PAWL'-sk'ee) Stuffed pike served whole on the platter. Originally a Polish dish.

икра из баклажан (ee-KRAH eez buh-kluh-ZHAHN) A relish composed of eggplant, onions, olives and oil.

лык (buh-LYK) Smoked fillet of sturgeon.

ранина (buh-RAH-n'i-nuh) Mutton.

Новороссийская баранина (nuh-vuh-ruhs-S'EES-kuh-yuh buh-RAH-n'i-nuh) Mutton cutlets baked with cabbage, carrots, turnips, potatoes, cauliflower, and seasonings.

вареники с творогом (vuh-R'EH-n'i-k'ee stvuh-ruh-GAWM). Pancakes stuffed with cream cheese, sour cream and eggs poached and served with melted butter and sour cream, or baked in the oven.

литовские вареники (l'i-TAWF-sk'i-yeh vuh-R'EH-n'k k'ee) Pancakes stuffed with chopped beef combined with kidney fat, chopped onions and a Béchamel sauce. A specialty of Lithuania.

ватрушки (vuh-TROOSH-k'ee) Small open tartlets of puff pastry filled with farmer's cheese.

вино́ (v'i-NAW) Wine.

крымское (KRYM-skuh-yeh) Crimean wine.

кавказское (kuhv-KAHZ-skuh-yeh) Caucasian wine.

бекас (b'i-KAHS) Snipe.

белуга (b'i-LOO-guh) *Beluga*, a very large variety of sturgeon from the Caspian Sea.

бёф строганов (b'awf STRAW-guh-nuhf) Strips of fillet of beef, sautéed with chopped onion and mushrooms, simmered with tomato juice and combined with sour cream.

биточки в сметане (b'i-TAWCH-k'ee fsm'i-TAH-n'eh) Russian meat balls in a sour-cream sauce.

блинчики (BL'EEN-chi-k'ee) Pancakes stuffed with various ingredients.

блинчики с сыром (BL'EEN-chi-k'ee SSY-ruhm) Ukrainian pancakes stuffed with a mixture of cream cheese, cottage cheese, egg yolks, sugar and vanilla, rolled up and fried in butter. Served either hot or cold.

блины (bl'i-NY) Buckwheat-flour pancakes, usually served with melted butter, sour cream, smoked salmon, herring, and sometimes caviar.

борщ (bawrshch) *Borscht*. A soup made with meat, fish or vegetable stock and sour beets. Often garnished with dumplings, sausage and meat. Served with sour cream.

борщ малороссийский (bawrshch muh-luh-ruhs-S'EE-sk'ee) A Ukrainian beet soup made with ham bone and beef stock, and containing pieces of beef, cubes of ham, and spicy sausage.

борщок (buhrsh-CHAWK) A thin beet soup with boiled potatoes, sprinkled with fresh dill and eaten with sour cream.

81

ртвинья (buht-V'EE-n'yuh) An originally Polish soup made with spinach, sorrel, beet tops, pickled beet juice, vinegar, white wine, chopped fennel and tarragon, cucumber, cold salmon, shrimp and horseradish. Served cold.

рынза (BRYN-zuh) A soft, slightly salted goat's cheese produced in the Ukraine and the Caucasus.

водка (VAWT-kuh) A highly alcoholic beverage made from rye, potatoes or maize. Almost tasteless, it should be gulped from small glasses, not sipped. Served with *zakuski*.

рябиновка (водка) (r'uh-B'EE-nuhf-kuh) Vodka flavored with bitter-sweet cherries bitten by frost.

зубровка (водка) (zoob-RAWF-kuh) Vodka flavored with buffalo grass.

перцовка (водка) (p'ir-TSAWF-kuh) Vodka infused with red pepper.

лимонная (водка) (l'ee-MAWN-nuh-yuh) Vodka flavored with lemon juice.

графинчик водки (gruh-F'EEN-chik VAWT-kee) A small carafe of vodka.

говядина (guh-V'AH-d'i-nuh) Beef.

голубцы (guh-loop-TS'EE) Stuffed cabbage.

грибы (gr'i-BY) Mushrooms.

грибы в сметане (gr'i-BY fsm'i-TAH-n'eh) Mushrooms with sour cream.

белые грибы (B'EH-ly-yeh gr'i-BY) White mushrooms.

маринованные грибы (muh-r'i-NAW-vuhn-ny-yeh gr'i-BY) Pickled mushrooms.

солёные грибы (suh-L'AW-ny-yeh gr'i-BY) Salted mushrooms.

грузди (grooz-D'EE) A type of black pepper-mushroom.

гусь (goos') Goose. The traditional Russian recipe calls for the goose to be roasted with apples.

драхона (druh-KHAW-nuh) A cake made with flour, milk, butter, eggs and sugar.

закуски (zuh-KOOS-k'ee) Hors d'oeuvres.

индейка с вишнёвым соусом (een-D'EY-kuh sv'ish-N'AW-vym SAW-oo-suhm) Thinly sliced breast of turkey, sautéed with butter and Madeira and served with a sauce made of pitted cherries, mixed spices and sugar.

капуста (kuh-POOS-tuh) Cabbage.

кислая капуста (K'EES-luh-yuh kuh-POOS-tuh) Sauerkraut.

каша (KAH-shuh) Buckwheat groats.

каша с грибами (KAH-shuh zgr'i-BAH-m'ee) Buckwheat *kasha* mixed with dried halved mushrooms and sour cream.

икра (ee-KRAH) Caviar.

кетовая *or* **красная икра** (k'i-TAW-vuh-yuh, KRAHS-nuh-yuh ee-KRAH) Salmon caviar.

малосольная икра (muh-luh-SAWL'-nuh-yuh ee-KRAH) Slightly salted caviar.

паюсная икра (PAH-yoos-nuh-yuh ee-KRAH) Pressed caviar, a rougher, saltier variety.

свежая икра (SV'EH-zhuh-yuh ee-KRAH) Unsalted fresh caviar. A large gray-grain caviar from the roe of the *beluga*, a very large species of sturgeon caught in the Caspian Sea. Cannot be exported; considered the best caviar.

холодная закуска (khuh-LAWD-nuh-yuh zuh-KOOS-kuh) Cold hors d'oeuvres.

горячая закуска (guh-R'AH-chuh-yuh zuh-KOOS-kuh) Hot hors d'oeuvres, usually served after cold hors d'oeuvres.

заливное (zuh-l'iv-NAW-yuh) Aspic with meat (pork, tongue, veal or ham), fish (usually sturgeon) or vegetables.

зразы с кашей (ZRAH-zy SKAH-shey) Sliced lean beef, rolled up with layers of *kasha* and fried onion, browned in butter, then simmered with a little stock.

паштет из зайца (puhsh-T'EHT eez ZEYE-tsuh) Chopped hare, made into a pie as above.

паштет из раков (puhsh-T'EHT eez RAH-kuhf) A shrimp-and-fish pie, made with peas, sour cream, lemon, and baked between layers of puff pastry.

пилав (p'i-LAHF) *or* плов (plawf) Pilaf.

пилав по кавказски (p'i-LAHF puh kuhf-KAHS-k'ee)
Sliced loin or leg of mutton, browned in mutton fat with
chopped onions, then simmered with stock and rice. A specialty
of the Caucasus.

пирог (p'i-RAWK) Pie. More frequently stuffed with meat
than with fruit.

пироженое (p'i-R'AW-zheh-nuh-yeh) French pastry.

пирожки (p'i-RAWSH-k'ee) Small individual pies stuffed
with meat, fish or vegetables, and fried in hot fat. Usually
served with soups.

пирожки из дичи (p'i-RAWSH-k'ee eez D'EE-chee) Puff-
pastry *piroshki* stuffed with minced cooked game, chopped
hard-cooked eggs, *kasha* or cooked rice, and butter, and baked
in the oven.

кавказские пирожки (kuhf-KAHS-k'i-yeh p'i-RAWSH-
k'ee) Small individual pies stuffed with cheese and mushrooms, bread crumbs and a Béchamel sauce, and fried in
boiling fat. A Caucasian specialty.

гречневая каша (GR'EHCH-n'ı-vuh-yuh KAH-shuh)
Sifted and slightly fried buckwheat groats, cooked in a slow
oven with salt and butter, and served like a cooked cereal, with
cream or melted butter.

квас (kvahs) A drink made by the simultaneous acid and
alcoholic fermentation of wheat, barley, rye, or buckwheat
meal, or even rye bread, with the addition of sugar or fruit.
Slightly alcoholic, it is sometimes added to soups.

кильки (K'EEL'-k'ee) Salted and marinated sardines.

кисель (k'i-S'EHL') A kind of sourish jelly made of linden-
berries or other berries.

колбаса (kuhl-buh-SAH) Sausage.

корюшка (KAW-r'oosh-kuh) Smelts.

жареная корюшка (ZHAH-r'i-nuh-yuh KAW-r'oosh-kuh)
Smelts cooked in chicken stock and butter, and flavored with
chopped shrimps and mushrooms.

маринованная корюшка (muh-r'ee-NAW-vuhn-nuh-yuh
KAW-r'oosh-kuh) Pickled smelts.

пельмени (p'il-M'EH-n'ee) Small pies.

пельмени по сибирски (p'il'-M'EH-n'ee puh s'i-B'EER-sk'ee) Small pies stuffed with finely chopped ham, pork, butter, lemon juice or vinegar and parsley, and poached, then served with melted butter and sour cream. Originally a Siberian specialty.

перепёлка (p'i-r'i-P'AWL-kuh) Quail.

(фаршированный) перец (fuhr-shy-RAW-vuhn-ny P'EH-r'its) Stuffed pepper.

печеная картофель в сметане (p'i-CHEH-nuh-yuh kuhr-TAW-f'il' fsm'i-TAH-n'eh) Sliced boiled potatoes baked with chopped onion, bread crumbs, grated cheese and sour cream.

пиво (P'EE-vuh) Beer.

котлеты (kuht-L'EH-ty) Rissoled forcemeat made with beef, chopped onion, and bread crumbs and kept in shape with an egg. Breaded and fried in butter. A variant is made with chopped salmon mixed with bread soaked in milk and butter; this is shaped into cutlets, browned in butter and served with a garnish of mushrooms, shrimps, slices of pickled cucumber, fresh peas and sour cream.

пожарские котлеты (puh-ZHAHR-sk'i-yeh kuht-L'EH-ty) Kotlety made with the meat of hazel hens, pork, bread soaked in milk, sour cream, butter and eggs.

крэм (krehm) Russian cream, somewhat like a Bavarian cream.

кулебяка (koo-l'i-B'AH-kuh) A sort of hot pie, consisting usually of spiced rice, meat, eggs, etc., arranged in layers.

кулебяка с сёмгой (koo-l'i-B'AH-kuh SS'AWM-goi) Sliced cooked salmon baked between layers of a paste made of flour, eggs, milk and sugar, to which other layers of kasha or cooked rice mixed with chopped onions and mushrooms have been added.

кулич (koo-L'EECH) An Easter bread made with currants, almonds and saffron.

пирожки с капустой (p'i-RAWSH-k'ee skuh-POOS-toi) Piroshki stuffed with finely shredded white cabbage that has been cooked in butter.

пудинг из чёрного хлеба с вишнями (POO-d'ink eez CHAWR-nuh-vuh KHL'EH-buh ZV'EESH-n'uh-m'ee) A pudding made of rye bread crumbs, cherries, eggs, almonds, butter, cinnamon and claret.

почки в сметане (PAWCH-k'ee fsm'i-TAH-n'eh) Thinly sliced lamb kidney, cooked in butter with chopped onion, flour, salt and pepper. Served with sour cream and fried potatoes.

раки (RAH-k'ee) Crayfish cooked in white wine with thyme and salt. A very delicate dish, extremely popular in Russia.

рассольник (ruhs-SAWL'-n'ik) A soup made with bouillon, onions, potatoes, pickles and sour cream, to which minced boiled beef kidney is added.

московские пирожки *or* разтягаи (muhs-KAWF-sk'i-yeh p'i-RAWSH-k'ee, ruhs-t'uh-GAH-ee) *Piroshki* stuffed with cooked whitefish, hard-cooked eggs and *vesiga* (the marrow from the backbone of the sturgeon), and baked in the oven. A Moscow specialty.

пирожки с рыбой (p'i-RAWSH-k'ee SRY-boi) *Piroshki* stuffed with fish, hard-cooked eggs and rice.

поросёнок (puh-ruh-S'AW-nuhk) Boiled jointed suckling pig, served with a sauce of sour cream, grated horseradish, salt and pepper.

поросёнок с кашей (puh-ruh-S'AW-nuhk SKAH-shey) Suckling pig stuffed with *kasha*, roasted and served with a sour-cream sauce.

редиска (в сметане) (r'i-D'EES-kuh fsm'i-TAH-n'eh) Radish (in sour cream). Russians eat radishes with butter and salt.

рябчик в сметане (R'AHP-chik fsm'i-TAH-n'eh) Roast hazel-grouse (*gelinotte*) in a sour-cream sauce with herbs and spices. Very plentiful in the northern regions and Siberia, and highly prized by gourmets.

солянка (suh-L'AHN-kuh) A sort of deep-dish pie made of meat or fish with sauerkraut and spices.

сосиски в томате (suh-S'EES-k'ee ftuh-MAH-t'eh) Skinned smoked sausages cut into small lengths and cooked in hot tomato sauce. Served on a hot dish.

суп (soop) Soup.

> литовский суп с клёцками (l'i-TAWF-sk'ee soop SKL'AWT-skuh-m'ee) A soup, originally from Livonia (Lithuania), made with beef stock, Béchamel, spinach, onions, sorrel and sour cream. The *klotski* are small dumplings made with chopped shallots, fennel and ham, and are added to¹ ·he soup before serving.

сыр (syr) Cheese.

сырники (SYR-n'i-k'ee) Small cakes whose chief ingredient is cheese.

творожники (tvuh-RAWZH-n'i-k'ee) Cream-cheese pancakes, made with cream cheese from sour cream or milk.

курица (KOO-r'i-tsuh) Chicken.

куропатка (koo-ruh-PAHT-kuh) Partridge.

лещ с кашей (l'ehshch SKAH-shey) Bream baked with *kasha*, chopped eggs, and herbs. Served with a sauce of sour cream and melted butter,

> лещ с хреном (l'ehshch SKHR'EH-nuhm) Bream boiled in vinegar, then poached with celery, leek, onions, and served with horseradish and lemon slices.

муссака (moos-suh-KAH) Chopped eggplant, onions, tomatoes and pieces of lamb fried separately, then mixed in a pan, sprinkled with grated cheese and heated in the oven. A specialty of Caucasus and the Ukraine.

мясо (M'AH-suh) Meat.

огурцы (uh-goor-TSY) Cucumbers.

окрошка (uh-KRAWSH-kuh) Boiled vegetables (beets, peas, carrots, potatoes, cucumbers or dill pickles, turnips) cubed and served in квас (*kvahs*).

салат из картофеля, фасоли и свёклы (suh-LAHT eez kuhr-TAW-f'i-l'uh, fuh-SAW-l'ee ee SV'AWK-ly) Cooked diced potatoes and beets, mixed with kidney beans and dressed with oil, vinegar, salt and pepper.

оладьи (uh-LAH-d'ee) Small pancakes made with milk, flour, yeast, butter, eggs, and served with sugar, jam or syrup.

омлет с грибам'. (uhm-L'EHT sgr'i-BAH-m'ee) An omelet made with mushrooms.

омлет со сметаной (uhm-L'EHT suh sm'i-TAH-noi) An omelet made with sour cream.

осетрина (uh-s'i-TR'EE-nuh) Sturgeon.

заливная осетрина (zuh-l'iv-NAH-yuh uh-s'i-TR'EE-nuh) Cold sturgeon served in a thick jellied broth and decorated with mayonnaise and cooked vegetables (carrots, cauliflower, etc.).

пастила (puh-st'ee-LAH) Fruit butter mixed with sugar, egg whites, rose water and powdered almonds, then baked in a slow oven.

пасха (PAHS-khuh) An Easter cake made with cream cheese, sour cream, butter, sugar, chopped almonds, candied peel and seeded raisins.

паштет из индейки (puhsh-T'EHT eez een-D'EY-k'ee) Turkey joints browned in butter, then stewed in wine, vinegar, chopped onion, lemon rind, parsley, dill, bay leaf, and peppercorns, and then covered with pie pastry with the addition of a forcemeat of veal, bacon, bread crumbs, chopped onions and capers, and baked.

салат латук со сметаной (suh-LAHT luh-TOOK suhsm'i-TAH-noi) Lettuce served with a dressing made of egg yolk, sugar, salt and pepper, sour cream, chopped fennel and sliced cucumber.

русский салат (ROOS-k'ee suh-LAHT) A salad made of cooked mixed vegetables and cooked meats, poultry, game or fish, seasoned with oil, vinegar, salt and pepper. (Often known as *vinaigrette*.)

свинина (zv'i-N'EE-nuh) Pork.

селёдка (s'i-L'AWT-kuh) Herring.

королевская селёдка (kuh-ruh-L'EHF-skuh-yuh s'i-L'AWT-kuh) Especially rich and tender fillets of herring, marinated and cured in olive oil.

маринованная селёдка (muh-r'i-NAW-vuhn-nuh-yuh s'i-L'AWT-kuh) Herring marinated with onions in white or red wine.

селёдка в белом вине (s'i-L'AWT-kuh VB'EH-luhm v'i-N'EH) Herring in white wine.

селёдка в сметане (s'i-L'AWT-kuh fsm'i-TAH-n'eh) Herring in sour cream, with onions.

сёмга (S'AWM-guh) Smoked fillet of salmon.

сиг (s'eek) Whitefish.

копчёный сиг (kuhp-CH'AW-ny s'eek) Smoked whitefish.

сливы (SL'EE-vy) Plums.

маринованные сливы и вишни (muh-r'i-NAW-vuhn-ny-yeh SL'EE-vy ee V'EESH-n'ee) Plums pickled with vinegar, sugar, cinnamon and cloves. Often served with game.

сметана (smi'-TAH-nuh) Sour cream.

сметанник (sm'i-TAHN-n'ik) A pie made with almonds, cherry and raspberry jam, sour cream, egg yolks and cinnamon.

снежки (sn'izh-K'EE) Stiffly beaten sweetened whites of eggs floating in a light custard.

угорь (OO-guhr') Eel.

копчёный угорь (kuhp-CH'AW-ny OO-guhr') Smoked eel.

утка (OOT-kuh) Duck.

уха (oo-KHAH) A fish soup, often made with sturgeon, perch or tench (but other fish may be used), onions, celery, parsley, fennel and peppercorns.

фазан (fuh-ZAHN) Pheasant.

форель в вине (fuh-R'EHL' v'i-N'EH) Trout simmered with fish stock, white wine, Madeira, rum, celery, leek, onion and mixed herbs. Served hot or cold.

хворост (KHVAW-ruhst) A thin, crisp pastry made with sugar, flour and, occasionally, vodka.

холодец (khuh-luh-D'EHTS) Pork in aspic, served with horseradish sauce.

чай heye) Tea.

11

HOTEL, BOARDINGHOUSE, APARTMENT

Where is a good (the best) hotel?

Где хороший (лучший) отель?

gd'eh khuh-RAW-shy (LOOCH-shy) uh-T'EHL'?

Here it is; it is in the center of the town (close to the station).

Вот тут; он в центре города (около станции).

vawt toot; awn FTS'EHN-tr'eh GAW-ruh-duh (AW-kuh-luh STAHN-ts'ee-i).

I want a front (back) room with twin beds.

Я хочу комнату с окнами на улицу (во двор) с двумя кроватями.

yah khuh-CHOO KAWM-nuh-too SAWK-nuh-m'ee nuh OO-l'i-tsoo (vuh DVAWR) sdvoo-M'AH kruh-VAH-t'uh-m'ee.

I want a suite near the elevator (near the stairs).

Я хочу квартиру около (возле) лифта (лестницы).

yah khuh-CHOO kvuhr-T'EE-roo AW-kuh-luh (VAWZ-l'eh) L'EEF-tuh (l'is-TN'EE-tsy).

I want a boardinghouse (furnished apartment, furnished room).

Я хочу (иметь) пансион (меблированную квартиру, меблированную комнату).

yah khuh-CHOO (ee-M'EHT') puhn-SYAWN (m'i-bl'i-RAW-vuhn-noo-yoo kvuhr-T'EE-roo, m'i-bl'i-RAW-vuhn-noo-yoo KAWM-nuh-too).

I want a living room, bedroom and kitchen.

Я хотел (хотела) бы иметь гостинную, спальню и кухню.

yah khuh-T'EL (khuh-T'EH-luh) by ee-M'EHT' guhs-T'EEN-noo-yoo, SPAHL'-n'oo ee KUKH-n'oo.

Are these rooms for rent?

Эти комнаты сдаются?

EH-t'ee KAWM-nuh-ty zduh-YOOT-suh?

Is it very expensive?

Он очень дорогой?

awn AW-chin' duh-ruh-GOI?

90

It is quite (not very) expensive.
Он довольно (не очень) дорогой.
awn duh-VAWL'-nuh (n'i AW-chin') duh-ruh-GOI.

Have you a single (double) room with bath?
Есть у вас комната для одного (для двух) с ванной?
yehst' oo vahs KAWM-nuh-tuh dl'uh uhd-nuh-VAW (dl'uh
    dvookh) SVAHN-noi?

  with shower
  с душем
  SDOO-shym

  with running water
  с текучей водой
  st'i-KOO-chey vuh-DOI

Have you a reservation?
Вы заказали заранее?
vy zuh-kuh-ZAH-l'ee zuh-RAH-n'i-yeh?

I made a reservation two weeks ago.
Я заказал (заказала) две недели тому назад.
yah zuh-kuh-ZAHL (zuh-kuh-ZAH-luh) dv'eh n'i-D'EH-l'ee
    tuh-MOO nuh-ZAHT.

How long are you staying?
Как долго вы останетесь?
kahk DAWL-guh vy uhs-TAH-n'ι-t'is'?

Overnight.
На ночь.
NAH-nawch'.

I shall be here till Saturday.
Я буду здесь до субботы.
yah BOO-doo zd'ehs' duh soob-BAW-ty.

I should like to see the room.
Я хотел (хотела) бы посмотреть комнату.
yah khuh-T'EHL (khuh-T'EH-luh) by puhs-muh-TR'EHT'
    KAWM-nuh-too.

I (don't) like this room.
Мне (не) нравится эта комната.
mn'eh (n'i) NRAH-v'it-suh EH-tuh KAWM-nuh-tuh.

It has no view.
Из неё нет никакого вида.
eez n'i-YAW n'cht n'i-kuh-KAW-vuh V'EE-duh.

91

The room faces the courtyard (the street).

Комната выходит на двор (на улицу).

KAWM-nuh-tuh vy-KHAW-d'it nuh dvawr (nuh OO-l'i-tsoo).

Have you something better (cheaper, larger)?

Нет ли у вас чего нибудь получше (дешевле, просторнее)?

n'eht l'i oo vahs chi-VAW-n'i-boot' puh-LOOCH-sheh (d'i-SHEHV-l'eh, pruhs-TAWR-n'i-yeh)?

How much is it by the day (week, month)?

Сколько в сутки (за неделю, за месяц)?

SKAWL'kuh FSOOT-k'ee (zuh n'i-D'EH-l'oo, zuh M'EH-s'uhts)?

On what floor is it?

На котором она этаже?

nuh kuh-TAW-ruhm uh-NAH eh-tuh-ZHEH?

On the third floor.

На третьем этаже.

nuh TR'EH-t'im eh-tuh-ZHEH.

Will you please sign the register?

Будьте добры (or любезны) расписаться.

BOOT'-t'eh duh-BRY (l'oo-B'EHZ-ny) ruh-sp'i-SAHT'-suh.

> **fill out the registration blank**
>
> заполнить регистрационный бланк
>
> zuh-PAWL-n'it' r'i-g'is-truh-TSYAWN-ny blahnk

May I reserve a room?

Могу ли я заказать комнату?

muh-GOO l'i yah zuh-kuh-ZAHT' KAWM-nuh-too?

May I leave my baggage here until Friday?

Могу ли я оставить свой багаж здесь до пятницы?

muh-GOO l'i yah uh-STAH-v'it' svoi buh-GAHSH zd'ehs' duh P'AHT-n'i-tsy?

Let me have my key, please.

Дайте пожалуйста ключ.

DEYE-t'eh puh-ZHAHL-stuh kl'ooch.

What is your room number?

Какой номер вашей комнаты?

kuh-KOI NAW-m'ir VAH-shey KAWM-nuh-ty?

Here is my (your) key.

Вот мой (ваш) ключ.

vawt moi (vahsh) kl'ooch.

It is too small (large, noisy, hot, cold).
Эна слишком мала (велика, шумная, жаркая, холодная).
ıh-NAH SL'EESH-kuhm muh-LAH (v'i-l'i-KAH, SHOOM-
nuh-yuh, ZHAHR-kuh-yuh, khuh-LAWD-nuh-yuh).

There is no rug (radio) in this room.
В комнате нет ковра (радио).
FKAWM-nuh-t'eh n'eht kuhv-RAH (RAH-d'ee-oh).

Are meals included?
Включая еду?
fkl'oo-CH'AH-yuh yi-DOO?

Only breakfast.
Только утренний чай.
TAWL'-kuh OO-tr'in-n'ee cheye.

How much is the room without meals?
Сколько стоит комната без еды?
SKAWL'-kuh STAW-yit KAWM-nuh-tuh b'ehz yi-DY?

How much do you charge for a room and three meals a day?
Сколько вы берёте за комнату с полным пансионом?
SKAWL'kuh vy b'i-R'AW-t'eh zuh KAWM-nuh-too SPAWL-
nym puhn-S'YAW-nuhm?

May I see your passport (your identification)?
Покажите пожалуйста ваш паспорт (ваше удостоверение).
puh-kuh-ZHY-t'eh puh-ZHAHL-stuh vahsh PAHS-puhrt
(VAH-sheh oo-duhs-tuh-v'i-R'EH-n'i-yeh).

There is no lock on the door.
В двери нет замка.
VDV'EH-r'ee n'eht zuhm-KAH.

Please draw the curtains.
Пожалуйста задёрните занавески.
puh-ZHAHL-stuh zuh-D'AWR-n'i-t'eh zuh-nuh-V'EHS-k'

Is there a hook here?
Есть ли тут крючёк?
YEHST'-li toot kr'oo-CHAWK?

When may I take a bath?
Когда я могу выкупаться?
kuhg-DAH yah muh-GOO VY-koo-puht'-suh?

I should like a bath tonight.
Я хотел (хотела) бы выкупаться сегодня вечером.
yah khuh-T'EHL (khuh-T'EH-luh) by VV-koo-puht'-suh s'i-
VAWD-n'uh V'EH-chi-ruhm.

Please send up a bellboy.
Пошлите мне пожалуйста корридорного.
puhsh-L'EE-t'eh mn'eh puh-ZHAHL-stuh kuhr-r'i-DAWR-
   nuh-vuh.

   a waiter
   слугу
   sloo-GOO

   a maid
   горничную
   GAWR-n'ich-noo-yoo

   some ice
   лёд
   l'awt

   some ice water
   воды со льдом
   vuh-DY suh-L'DAWM

Where is the bathroom?
Где ванная комната?
gd'eh VAHN-nuh-yuh KAWM-nuh-tuh?

   the telephone
   телефон
   t'i-l'i-FAWN

   the lavatory
   уборная
   oo-BAWR-nuh-yuh

   the dining room
   столовая
   stuh-LAW-vuh-yuh

Where is the electric switch?
Где выключатель?
gd'eh vy-kl'oo-CHAH-t'ehl'?

   the outlet
   штепсельная коробка
   SHT'EHP-s'il'-nuh-yuh kuh-RAWP-kuh

   the closet
   чулан
   choo-LAHN

94

the lamp
лампа
LAHM-puh

the wash basin
умывальник
oo-my-VAHL'-n'ik

Please send to my room another pillow.
Пошлите пожалуйста ко мне в комнату лишнюю подушку.
puhsh-L'EE-t'eh puh-ZHAHL-stuh kuh mn'eh FKAWM-nuh-
  too L'EESH-n'oo-yoo puh-DOOSH-koo.

another blanket
лишнее одеяло
L'EESH-n'i-yeh uh-d'i-YAH-luh

another hanger
лишнюю вешалку
L'EESH-n'oo-yoo V'EH-shuhl-koo

soap
мыло
MY-luh

toilet paper
туалетную бумагу
too-uh-L'EHT-noo-yoo boo-MAH-goo

There are mosquitoes on the wall (ceiling).
Тут комары на стене (на потолке).
toot kuh-muh-RY nuh st'i-N'EH (nuh puh-tuhl-K'EH).

Please spray.
Попрыскайте пожалуйста.
puh-PRY-skeye-t'eh puh-ZHAHL-stuh.

Let me have a mosquito net (bathmat).
Дайте мне сетку от комаров (ванный коврик).
DEYE-t'eh mn'eh S'EHT-koo uht kuh-muh-RAWF (VAHN-ny
  KAW-vr'ik).

What is that for?
Для чего это?
dl'uh chi-VAW EH-tuh?

Shall I leave them outside the door?
Можно их выставить за дверь?
MAWZH-nuh eekh VY-stuh-v'it' zuh dv'ehr'?

You must provide your own soap and sponge.

Вы должны запастись своим мылом и губкой.

vy duhl-ZHNY zuh-puh-ST'EES' svuh-YIM MY-luhm ee GOOP-koi.

I want my shoes shined.

Я хочу, чтобы мне вычистили ботинки.

yah khuh-CHOO SHTAW-by mn'eh VY-chis-t'i-lee buh-T'EEN-k'ee.

Send these things to the laundry (cleaner's).

Пошлите эти вещи в прачечную (в чистку).

puhsh-L'EE-t'eh EH-t'ee V'EHSH-chee FPRAH-chich-noo-yoo (FCHEEST-koo).

When do I get them back?

Когда я получу их обратно?

kuhg-DAH yah puh-loo-CHOO eekh uh BRAHT-nuh?

Have this suit pressed.

Прогладьте этот костюм.

pruh-GLAHT'-t'eh EH-tuht kuh-ST'OOM.

I want it back tonight.

Я хочу получить его обратно сегодня вечером.

yah khuh-CHOO puh-loo-CHEET' yi+VAW uh-BRAHT-nuh s'i-VAWD-n'uh V'EH-chi-ruhm.

Please change the sheets (pillowcases, towels).

Перемените пожалуйста простыни (наволочки, полотенца).

p'i-r'i-m'i-N'EE-t'eh puh-ZHAHL-stuh PRAW-sty-n'ee (NAH-vuh-luhch-k'ee, puh-luh-T'EHN-tsuh).

The water is not hot.

Вода не горячая.

vuh-DAH n'eh guh-R'AH-chuh-yuh.

I want to speak to the manager.

Я хотел (хотела) бы поговорить с управляющим.

yah khuh-T'EHL (khuh-T'EH-luh) by puh-guh-vuh-R'EET' soo-pruh-VL'AH-yoosh-chim.

Where is the ashtray (sink, tap)?

Где пепельница (слив, кран)?

gd'eh P'EH-p'ii'-n'i-tsuh (sl'eef, krahn)?

Open the window.

Откройте окно.

uht-KROI-t'eh uhk-NAW.

96

Close the door.
Закройте дверь.
zuh-KROI-t'eh dv'ehr'.

May I come in?
Можно войти?
MAWZH-nuh voi-T'EE?

Come in!
Войдите!
voi-D'EE-t'eh!

Who is there?
Кто там?
ktaw tahm?

Wait a minute!
Подождите минуту
puh-duhzh-D'EE-t'eh m'i-NOO-too!

Do not disturb.
Не беспокойте.
n'eh b'is-puh-KOI-t'eh.

Call me at 6 a.m.
Разбудите меня в шесть часов утра.
ruhz-boo-D'EE-t'eh m'i-N'AH fshehst' chuh-SAWF oo-TRAH.

Are there any letters (parcels) for me?
Есть ли для меня письма (пакеты)?
YEHST'-l'i dl'uh m'i-N'AH P'EES'-muh (puh-K'EH-ty)?

Ask the doorman.
Спросите швейцара.
spruh-S'EE-t'eh shv'ey-TSAH-ruh.

Here is a letter for you.
Вот письмо для вас.
vawt p'is'-MAW dl'uh vahs.

There is no mail.
Почты нету.
PAWCH-ty N'EH-too.

Did anyone call me?
Звонил ли кто нибудь мне?
zvuh-N'EEL l'i KTAW-n'i-boot' mn'eh?

Did anyone come for me?
Приходил ли кто нибудь ко мне?
pr'i-khuh-D'EEL l'i KTAW-n'i-boot' kuh mn'eh?

No one called.
Никто не звонил.
n'i-KTAW n'eh zvuh-N'EEL.

No one came.
Никто не приходил.
n'i-KTAW n'eh pr'i-khuh-D'EEL.

There is someone to see you.
Здесь кто то хочет вас видеть.
zd'ehs' KTAW-tuh KHAW-cheht vahs V'EE-d'eht'.

If someone calls, tell him I'll be back at three.
Если кто нибудь мне позвонит, скажите, что я буду в три
часа.
YEHS-l'i KTAW-n'i-boot' mn'eh puhz-vuh-N'EET, skuh-
ZHY-t'eh, shtuh yah BOO-doo ftr'ee chuh-SAH.

I'm expecting someone; tell him to wait.
Я ожидаю кое кого; попросите его подождать меня.
yah uh-zhy-DAH-yoo KAW-yeh kuh-VAW; puh-pruh-S'EE-
t'eh yi-VAW puh-duhzh-DAHT' m'i-N'AH.

Put this package on the table.
Положите этот пакет на стол.
puh-luh-ZHY-t'eh EH-tuht puh-K'EHT nuh stawl.

   on the chair
   на стул
   nuh stool

   on the armchair
   на кресло
   nuh KR'EH-sluh

   on the sofa
   на диван
   nuh d'i-VAHN

I'm checking out at 6 a.m.
Я уезжаю в шесть часов утра.
yah oo-yiz-ZHAH-yoo fshehst' chuh-SAWF oo-TRAH.

Please prepare my bill.
Приготовьте пожалуйста счёт.
pr'i-guh-TAWF'-t'eh puh-ZHAHL-stuh schawt.

Is everything included?
Сюда входит всё?
s'oo-DAH FKHAW-d'it fs'aw?

The service and tax are included.
Услуги и такса входят.
oo-SLOO-g'ee ee TAHK-suh FKHAW-d'uht.

Forward my mail to this address.
Перешлите мою почту по этому адресу.
p'i-r'ish-L'EE-t'eh muh-YOO PAWCH-too puh EH-tuh-moo
   AH-dr'i-soo.

Hold my mail until I return.
Задержите мои письма до моего возвращения.
zuh-d'ir-ZHY-t'eh muh-EE P'EES'-muh duh muh-yi-VAW
   vuhz-vruhsh-CHEH-n'ee-yuh.

Please give me stamps.
Дайте мне пожалуйста марок.
DEYE-t'eh mn'eh puh-ZHAHL-stuh MAH-ruhk.

   writing paper
   писчей бумаги
   P'EES-chey boo-MAH-g'ee

   envelopes
   конвертов
   kuhn-V'EHR-tuhf

   post cards
   открыток
   uht-KRY-tuhk

I want an interpreter (guide, secretary) **who speaks English.**
Я хотел (хотела) бы переводчика (гида, секретаря) который
   говорит по-английски
yah khuh-T'EHL (khuh-T'EH-luh) by p'i-r'i-VAWT-chi-kuh
   (G'EE-duh, s'i-kr'i-tuh-R'AH), kuh-TAW-ry guh-vuh-R'EET
   puh-uhn-GL'EE-sk'ee

Page Mr. Orloff in the lobby.
Позовите гражданина Орлова в передней.
puh-zuh-V'EE-t'eh gruh-zh-duh-N'EE-nuh uhr-LAW-vuh fp'i-
   R'EHD-n'ey.

12

MEDICAL, DENTAL, DRUGSTORE, PARTS OF THE BODY

Where can I find a good doctor (surgeon, dentist, oculist)?
Где могу я найти хорошего доктора (хирурга, дантиста, окулиста)?
gd'eh muh-GOO yah neye-T'EE khuh-RAW-shy-vuh DAWK-tuh-ruh (khee-ROOR-guh, duhn-T'EES-tuh, uh-koo-L'EES-tuh)?

Here is Dr. Orlov's address.
Вот адрес доктора Орлова.
vawt AH-dr'is DAWK-tuh-ruh uhr-LAW-vuh.

I am ill (indisposed).
Я болен (больна) (нездоров) (нездорова).
yah BAW-l'in (buhl'-NAH) (n'i-zduh-RAWF) (n'i-zduh-RAW-vuh).

I have a cold (head cold).
У меня простуда (насморк).
oo m'i-N'AH pruh-STOO-duh (NAHS-muhrk).

    cough кашель KAH-shyl'

    headache головная боль guh-luhv-NAH-yuh bawl'

    stomach-ache болит живот buh-L'EET zhy-VAWT

    toothache болит зуб buh-L'EET zoop

    indigestion расстройство ruhs-STROIST-vuh

    abscess нарыв nuh-RYF

    sore throat болит горло buh-L'EET GAWR-luh

I think I may have dysentery (seasickness).
Я думаю, что у меня дезинтерия (морская болезнь).
yah DOO-muh-yoo, shtaw oo m'i-N'AH d'i-z'in-T'EH-r'i-yuh (muhr-SKAH-yuh buh-L'EHZN').

Please call a doctor (nurse).

Позовите пожалуйста доктора (сестру милосердия).

puh-zuh-V'EE-t'eh puh-ZHAHL-stuh DAWK-tuh-ruh (s'is-
  TROO m'i-luh-S'EHR-d'i-yuh).

Take off your clothes (to the waist).

Разденьтесь (до пояса).

ruhz-D'EHN'-t'ehs' (duh PAW-yuh-suh).

Lie down.

Лягте.

L'AHK-t'eh.

Open your mouth.

Откройте рот.

uht-KROI-t'eh rawt.

Let me see your tongue.

Дайте посмотреть ваш язык.

DEYE-t'eh puh-smuh-TR'EHT' vahsh yuh-ZYK.

Breathe hard.

Вздохните глубоко.

vzduhkh-N'EE-t'eh gloo-buh-KAW.

The skin is broken.

Кожа повреждена.

KAW-zhuh puh-vr'izh-d'i-NAH.

Have you lost much blood?

Вы потеряли много крови?

vy puh-t'i-R'AH-l'ee MNAW-guh kruh-V'EE?

I have a pain in my chest.

У меня боль в груди.

oo m'i-N'AH BAWL' vgroo-D'EE.

  in my hand
  в руке
  vroo-K'EH

  in my foot
  в ноге
  vnuh-G'EH

  in my shoulder
  в плече
  fpl'i-CHEH

in my ankle
в щиколотке
FSHCHEE-kuh-luht-k'eh

in my finger
в пальце
FPAHL'-ts'eh

in my thumb
в большом пальце
vbuhl-SHAWM PAHL'-ts'eh

My arm hurts.
У меня болит рука.
oo m'i-N'AH buh-L'EET roo-KAH.

leg нога nuh-GAH

back спина sp'i-NAH

neck шея SHEH-yuh

ear ухо OO-khuh

eye глаз glahs

nose нос naws

face лицо l'i-TSAW

lip губа goo-BAH

cheek щека shchi-KAH

head голова guh-luh-VAH

Where does it hurt?
Где болит?
gd'eh buh-L'EET?

Here.
Здесь.
zd'ehs.

I am dizzy.
У меня кружится голова.
oo m'i-N'AH KROO-zhyt-suh guh-luh-VAH.

Are you nauseated?
Вас тошнит?
vahs tuhsh-N'EET?

No, but my forehead is hot and I have chills (fever).
Нет, но у меня горячий лоб и меня знобит (лихорадит).
n'eht, nuh oo m'i-N'AH guh-R'A-chy lawp ee m'i-N'AH znuh-
B'EET (l'i-khuh-RAH-d'it).

How long have you had this pain?
С какого времени у вас эта боль?
skuh-KAW-vuh VR'EH-m'i-n'i oo vahs EH-tuh BAWL'?

Since yesterday.
Со вчерашнего дня.
suh fcheh-RAHSH-n'i-vuh dn'ah.

Let me examine your right eye.
Дайте мне посмотреть ваш правый глаз.
DEYE-t'eh mn'eh puh-smuh-TR'EHT' vahsh PRAH-vy glahs.

Your heart and lungs are O.K.
Ваше сердце и лёгкие в порядке.
VAH-sheh S'EHRT-tseh ee L'AWKH-k'yeh fpuh-R'AHT-
k'eh.

The bone (rib) is broken.
Кость (ребро) сломана (сломано).
kawst' (r'i-BRAW) SLAW-muh-nuh (SLAW-muh-nuh).

The wrist is sprained.
Запястье вывихнуто.
zuh-P'AHS-t'eh VY-v'ikh-noo-tuh.

I broke a finger (toe) nail.
У меня сломан ноготь на пальце (на пальце ноги).
oo m'i-N'AH SLAW-muhn NAW-guht' nuh PAHL'-ts'eh (nuh
PAHL'-ts'eh nuh-G'EE).

You have a fracture (bruise, cut, burn).
У вас перелом (синяк, рана, ожёг).
oo vahs p'i-r'i-LAWM (s'i-N'AHK, RAH-nuh, uh-ZHAWK).

Do I have to go to the hospital?
Должен (должна) ли я отправиться в больницу?
DAWL-zhyn (duhlzh-NAH) l'i yah uht-PRAH-v'it'-suh vbuhl'-
N'EE-tsoo?

No, but you must stay in bed.
Нет, но вы должны остаться в кровати.
n'eht, nuh vy duhlzh-NY uh-STAHT'-suh fkruh-VAH-t'ee.

Do you feel better today?

Чувствуете ли вы себя лучше сегодня?

CHOOFS-tvoo-yi-t'eh l'i vy s'i-B'AH LOOCH-sheh s'i-VAWD-n'ah?

No, I feel worse.

Нет, я чувствую себя хуже.

n'eht, yah CHOOFS-tvoo-yoo s'i-B'AH KHOO-zheh.

How often must I take this medicine?

Как часто я должен (должна) принимать это лекарство?

kahk CHAHS-tuh yah DAWL-zhyn (duhlzh-NAH) pr'i-n'i-MAHT' EH-tuh l'i-KAHRST-vuh?

One spoonful every two hours.

Одну полную ложку каждые два часа.

uhd-NOO PAWL-noo-yoo LAWZH-koo KAHZH-dy-yeh dvah chuh-SAH.

Take one pill with a glass of water three times a day before (after) meals.

Принимайте по одной пилюле в стакане воды три раза в день перед едой (после еды).

pr'i-n'i-MEYE-t'eh puh uhd-NOI p'i-L'OO-l'eh fstuh-KAH-n'eh vuh-DY tr'ee RAH-zuh vd'ehn' P'EH-r'id yi-DOI (PAWS-l'eh yi-DY)

You smoke too much.

Вы курите слишком много.

vy KOO-r'i-t'eh SL'EESH-kuhm MNAW-guh.

Stop smoking for a few days.

Не курите несколько дней.

n'i koo-R'EE-t'eh N'EH-skuhl'-kuh dn'ey.

I cannot move my elbow (knee).

Я не могу двигать локотем (коленом).

yah n'i muh-GOO DV'EE-guht' LAW-kuh-t'ehm (kuh-L'EH-nuhm).

Your hand is swollen.

Ваша рука распухла.

VAH-shuh roo-KAH ruhs-POOKH-luh.

I have lost a filling.

У меня выпала пломба.

oo m'i-N'AH VY-puh-luh PLAWM-buh.

104

Can you fill it?
Можете ли вы его запломбировать?
MAW-zhy-t'eh l'i vy yi-VAW zuh-pluhm-B'EE-ruh-vuht'?

Can you repair this denture?
Можете ли вы поправить эти искуственные зубы?
MAW-zhy-t'eh l'i vy puh-PRAH-v'it' EH-t'i ees-KOOST-v'in-
ny-yeh ZOO-by?

How long will it take?
Сколько времени нужно на это?
SKAWL'-kuh VR'EH-m'i-n'i NOOZH-nuh nuh EH-tuh?

I have broken my glasses.
Я поломал (поломала) очки.
yah puh-luh-MAHL (puh-luh-MAH-luh) uhch-K'EE.

Can you put in a new lens?
Можете ли вы вставить новые стёкла?
MAW-zhy-t'eh l'i vy FSTAH-v'it' NAW-vy-yeh ST'AW-kluh?

Where is a drugstore?
Где аптека?
gd'eh uhp-T'EH-kuh?

Have you a prescription?
Есть у вас рецепт?
yehst' oo vahs r'i-TSEHRPT?

Give me the aspirin.
Дайте мне аспирин.
DEYE-t'eh mn'eh uh-sp'i-R'EEN.

  iodine иод yawt

  a mild laxative лёгкое слабительное L'AWKH-kuh-yeh
    sluh-B'EE-t'il'-nuh-yeh

  gauze марлю MAHR-l'oo

  a bandage бинт b'eent

  a thermometer термометр t'ir-MAW-m'itr

  adhesive tape пластырь PLAHS-tyr'

  absorbent cotton вату VAH-too

  talcum powder тальк в порошке tahl'k fpuh-ruhsh-
    K'EH

105

bicarbonate of soda соду бикарбоник SAW-doo b'i-kuhr-BAW-n'ik

quinine tablets хину в таблетках KHEE-noo ftuh-BL'EHT-kuhkh

cough syrup сироп от кашля s'i-RAWP uht KAHSH-l'uh

boric acid борную кислоту BAWR-noo-yoo k'is-luh-TOO

castor oil касторовое масло kuh-STAW-ruh-vuh-yeh MAHS-luh

When can I travel?
Когда могу я ехать?
kuhg-DAH muh-GOO yah YEH-khuht'?

Not until next Monday.
Не раньше следующего понедельника.
n'i RAHN'-shy SL'EH-doo-yoosh-chi-vuh puh-n'i-D'EHL'-n'i-kuh.

My gums hurt me.
У меня болят дёсны.
oo m'i-N'AH buh-L'AHT D'AWS-ny.

This tooth should be extracted.
Этот зуб нужно удалить.
EH-tuht zoop NOOZH-nuh oo-duh-L'EET'.

The X ray shows an abscess at the root.
Рентген показывает нарыв у корня.
r'int-G'EHN puh-KAH-zy-vuh-yit nuh-RYF oo KAWR-n'uh.

(To change from Fahrenheit to Centigrade, subtract 32 and multiply by 5/9; to change from Centigrade to Fahrenheit, multiply by 9/5 and add 32. Russian thermometers are usually of the Centigrade variety, and Soviet doctors and nurses normally record patients' body temperature in Centigrade.)

13

LAUNDRY, DRY CLEANING, BARBERSHOP, BEAUTY SALON

I have something to be washed.
У меня есть кое что выстирать.
oo m'i-N'AH yehst' KAW-yi-shtaw VYS-t'i-ruht'.

pressed прогладить pruh-GLAH-d'it'

brushed вычистить VY-chis-t'it'

mended починить puh-chi-N'EET'

dry-cleaned для химической чистки dl'uh khi-M'EE-chis-koi CHEEST-k'ee

Please send the valet up to my room.
Пошлите пожалуйста слугу ко мне в комнату.
puhsh-L'EE-t'eh puh-ZHAHL-stuh sloo-GOO kuh mn'eh FKAWM-nuh-too.

Here is the list:
Тут список:
toot SP'EE-suhk:

five shirts пять рубашек p'aht' roo-BAH-shyk

six handkerchiefs шесть носовых платков shehst' nuh-suh-VYKH pluht-KAWF

four pairs of socks четыре пары носков chi-TY-r'i PAH-ry nuhs-KAWF

six shorts шесть трусиков shehst' TROO-s'i-kuhf

one blouse одна блуза uhd-NAH BLOO-zuh

two pajamas две пижамы dv'eh p'i-ZHAH-my

one suit один костюм uh-D'EEN kuhs-T'OOM

one overcoat одно пальто uhd-NAW puhl'-TAW

two ties два галстуха dvah GAHLS-too-khuh

one sweater   одна фуфайка   uhd-NAH foo-FEYE-kuh

one pair of gloves   одна пара перчаток   uhd-NAH PAH-ruh p'ir-CHAH-tuhk

two woollen dresses   два шерстянных платья   dvah shyr-st'uhn-NYKH PLAH-t'uh

(Don't) starch the collars of the shirts.
(Не крахмальте) подкрахмальте воротнички у рубашек.
(n'i kruhkh-MAHL'-t'eh) puht-krukh-MAHL'-t'eh vuh-ruht-n'ich-K'EE oo roo-BAH-shyk.

(Don't) use bleach.
(Не) употребляйте белила.
(n'i) oo-puh-tr'ib-L'EYE-t'eh b'i-L'EE-luh.

When will you bring it back?
Когда вы это вернёте?
kuhg-DAH vy EH-tuh v'ir-N'AW-t'eh?

I need it tonight.
Мне это нужно сегодня вечером.
mn'eh EH-tuh NOOZH-nuh s'i-VAWD-n'uh V'EH-chi-ruhm.

I'm leaving tomorrow.
Я уезжаю завтра.
yah oo-yiz-ZHAH-yoo ZAHF-truh.

The belt (a button) is missing.
Недостаёт пояса (пуговицы).
n'i-duh-stuh-YAWT PAW-yuh-suh (POO-guh-v'i-tsy).

Try to find it.
Постарайтесь найти это.
puh-stuh-REYE-t'is' neye-T'EE EH-tuh.

This suit is not properly cleaned.
Костюм неважно вычищен.
kuhs-T'OOM n'i-VAHZH-nuh VY-chish-chin.

Can't you get it cleaner?
Не можете ли вы вычистить лучше?
n'i MAW-zhy-t'eh l'i vy VY-chis-t'it' LOOCH-sheh?

Where is there a good barbershop (beauty salon)?
Где тут хорошая парикмахерская (дамская парикмахерская)?
gd'eh toot khuh-RAW-shuh-yuh puh-r'ik-MAH-khir-skuh-yuh
(DAHM-skuh-yuh puh-r'ik-MAH-khir-skuh-yuh)?

Please give me a haircut (shave).
Пожалуйста постригите (побрейте) меня.
puh-ZHAHL-stuh puh-str'i-G'EE-t'eh (puh-BR'EY-t'eh) m'i-
N'AH.

Don't cut it too short.
Не стригите слишком коротко.
n'i str'i-G'EE-t'eh SL'EESH-kuhm KAW-ruht-kuh.

Where do you part your hair?
Где вы делаете пробор?
gd'eh vy D'EH-leye-t'eh pruh-BAWR?

In the middle.
Посредине.
puhs-r'i-D'EE-n'eh.

More to the side.
Больше в сторону.
BAWL'-sheh FSTAW-ruh-noo.

(Don't) use clippers.
(Не) употребляйте машинки.
(n'i) oo-puh-tr'i-BL'EYE-t'eh muh-SHEEN-k'ee.

Use the scissors.
Пользуйтесь ножницами.
PAWL'-zooy-t'ehs NAWZH-n'i-tsuh-m'i.

Here's a mirror.
Вот зеркало.
vawt Z'EHR-kuh-luh.

Cut off more at the side (back).
Подстригите больше со стороны (сзади).
puhd-str'i-G'EE-t'eh BAWL'-sheh suh-stuh-ruh-NY (SZAH-
d'i).

Don't cut at the top.
Не стригите на темени.
n'i str'i-G'EE-teh nuh T'EH-m'i-n'i.

Do you want hair tonic (pomade)?
Желаете элексир (помаду) для волос?
zhy-LAH-yi-t'eh eh-l'ik-S'EER (puh-MAH-doo) dl'uh vuh-
LAWS?

   a scalp massage массаж головы muhs-SAHZH guh-
luh-VY

a facial massage массаж лица muhs-SAHZH l'i-TSAH

a shampoo шампунь shuhm-POON'

a permanent перманентную завивку p'ir-muh-N'EHNT-noo-yoo zuh-V'EEF-koo

Is there a manicurist (chiropodist) here?
Делают ли здесь маникюр (педикюр)?
D'EH-luh-yoot l'i zd'ehs muh-n'i-K'OOR (p'i-d'i-K'OOR)?

I want my hair washed, set and tinted.
Я хотела бы помыть голову, привести в порядок волосы и покрасить их.
yah khuh-T'EH-luh by puh-MYT' GAW-luh-voo, pr'i-v'is-T'EE fpuh-R'AH-duhk VAW-luh-sy ee puh-KRAH-s'it' eekh.

The water is too hot (cold).
Вода слишком горяча (холодна).
vuh-DAH SL'EESH-kuhm guh-r'uh-CHAH (khuh-luhd-NAH).

Where can I get my shoes repaired?
Где можно починить ботинки?
gd'eh MAWZH-nuh puh-chi-N'EET' buh-T'EEN-k'ee?

I want rubber (leather) lifts (half soles).
Я хочу резиновые (кожанные) стельки (полуподмётки).
yah khuh-CHOO r'i-Z'EE-nuh-vy-yeh (KAW-zhuhn-ny-yeh) ST'EHL'-k'ee (puh-loo-puhd-M'AWT-k'ee).

14

SHOPPING

I should like to go shopping today.
Я хотел (хотела) бы пойти сегодня за покупками.
yah khuh-T'EHL (khuh-T'EH-luh) by poi-T'EE s'i-VAWD-
n'uh zuh puh-KOOP-kuh-m'ee.

I should like to go to a ladies' (men's) clothing store.
Я хотел (хотела) бы пойти в магазин дамского (мужского)
платья.
yah khuh-T'EHL (khuh-T'EH-luh) by poi-T'EE vmuh-guh-
Z'EEN DAHM-skuh-vuh (moosh-SKAW-vuh) PLAH-t'uh.

   to a department store в универмаг voo-n'i-v'ir-MAHK

   to a hat shop в шляпный магазин FSHL'AHP-ny muh-
   guh-Z'EEN

   to a shoe shop в магазин обуви vmuh-guh-Z'EEN AW-
   boo-v'ee

   to the tailor's к портному kpuhrt-NAW-moo

   to the jeweler's к ювелиру kyoo-v'i-L'EE-roo

   to a bookstore в книжный магазин FKN'EEZH-ny
   muh-guh-Z'EEN

   to a perfume shop в парфюмерный магазин fpuhr-f'oo-
   M'EHR-ny muh-guh-Z'EEN

   to a cigar store в табачный магазин ftuh-BAHCH-ny
   muh-guh-Z'EEN

   to a stationer's в писчебумажный магазин fp'is-chi-boo-
   MAHZH-ny muh-guh-Z'EEN

There's an interesting sale today at GUM.
Сегодня интересная распродажа в Гуме.
s'i-VAWD-n'uh een-t'i-R'EHS-nuh-yuh ruhs-pruh-DAH-zhuh
VGOO-m'eh.

111

May I help you?
Могу я вам помочь?
muh-GOO yah vahm puh-MAWCH'?

What do you want?
Что вы хотите?
shtaw vy khuh-T'EE-t'eh?

I want a felt hat.
Я хотел (хотела) бы фётровую шляпу.
yah khuh-T'EHL (khuh-T'EH-luh) by F'AW-truh-voo-yoo
SHL'AH-poo.

    a straw hat соломенную шляпу suh-LAW-m'in-noo-yoo
    SHL'AH-poo

    a suit костюм kuhs-T'OOM

    a tie галстух GAHL-stookh

    a dress платье PLAH-t'eh

    a scarf шарф shahrf

    a skirt юбку YOOP-koo

    a slip дамскую рубашку DAHMS-koo-yoo roo-BAHSH-
    koo

    a coat пиджак p'id-ZHANK

    pants брюки BR'OO-k'ee

    a vest жилет zhy-L'EHT

    a bra бюстгальтер b'oost-GAHL'-t'ir

    a girdle корсет kuhr-S'EHT

    sandals сандалии suhn-DAH-l'ee-i

    rubbers калоши kuh-LAW-shy

    a belt пояс PAW-yuhs

    a bathrobe купальный халат koo-PAHL'-ny khuh-
    LAHT

    a raincoat дождевик duhzh-d'i-V'EEK

    a shawl шаль shahl'

    a piece of cloth кусок материи koo-SAWK muh-T'EH-
    r'ee-i

an overcoat пальто puhl'-TAW

a wallet бумажник boo-MAHZH-n'ik

an umbrella дождевой зонтик duhzh-d'i-VOI ZAWN-t'ik

a parasol зонтик от солнца ZAWN-t'ik uht SAWN-tsuh

a bathing suit купальный костюм koo-PAHL'-ny kuhs-T'OOM

a bathing cap купальную шапочку koo-PAHL'-noo-yoo SHAH-puhch-koo

a handkerchief носовой платок nuh-suh-VOI pluh-TAWK

a robe халат khuh-LAHT

a blouse блузу BLOO-zoo

a shirt рубашку roo-BAHSH-koo

a sweater фуфайку foo-FEYE-koo

underwear нижнее бельё N'EEZH-n'i-yeh b'i-L'AW

a handbag сумочку SOO-muhch-koo

thread нитки N'EET-k'ee

darning cotton штопальные нитки SHTAW-puhl'-ny-yeh N'EET-k'ee

a cap шапку SHAHP-koo

a nightgown ночную рубашку nuhch-NOO-yoo roo-BAHSH-koo

Where do they sell gloves?
Где продаются перчатки?
gd'eh pruh-duh-YOOT-suh p'ir-CHAHT-k'ee?

pins булавки boo-LAHF-k'ee

needles иголки ee-GAWL-k'ee

diapers пелёнки p'i-L'AWN-k'ee

slippers туфли TOOF-l'ee

shorts трусики, кальсоны TROO-s'i-k'ee, kuhl'-SAW-ny

113

shoes обувь AW-boof'

socks носки nuhs-K'EE

stockings чулки chool-K'EE

garters подвязки puhd-V'AHS-k'ee

suspenders подтяжки puht-T'AHSH-k'ee

panties панталоны (*or* трико) puhn-tuh-LAW-ny (tr'ee-KAW)

pajamas пижамы p'i-ZHAH-my

What size (color)?
Какой размер (цвет)?
kuh-KOI ruhz-M'EHR (tsv'eht)?

Do you have it in black?
Есть ли у вас это чёрного цвета?
YEHST'-l'i oo vahs EH-tuh CHAWR-nuh-vuh TSV'EH-tuh?

in white белого B'EH-luh-yuh

in green зелёного z'i-L'AW-nuh-vuh

in blue синего S'EE-n'i-vuh

in red красного KRAHS-nuh-vuh

in brown коричневого kuh-R'EECH-n'i-vuh-vuh

in yellow жёлтого ZHAWL-tuh-vuh

in pink розового RAW-zuh-vuh-vuh

in gray серого S'EH-ruh-vuh

in tan беж b'ehsh

in purple лилового цвета l'i-LAW-vuh-vuh TSV'EH-tuh

in lilac сиреневого s'i-R'EH-n'i-vuh-vuh

I (do not) like this color.
Мне (не) нравится этот цвет.
mn'eh (n'ch) NRAH-v'i-tsuh EH-tuht tsv'eht.

I (do not) like this size.
Мне (не) подходит этот размер.
mn'eh (n'eh) puht-KHAW-d'it EH-tuht ruhz-M'EHR.

114

This is cheap (expensive).
Это дёшево (дорого).
EH-tuh D'AW-shy-vuh (DAW-ruh-guh).

Do you have anything cheaper (better, more expensive)?
Есть ли у вас что либо дешевле (лучше, дороже)?
YEHST'-l'i oo vahs SHTAW-l'i-buh d'i-SHEHV-l'eh
(LOOCH-sh'eh, duh-RAW-zheh)?

Do you have anything larger?
Нет ли у вас чего нибудь побольше?
N'EHT-l'i oo vahs chi-VAW-n'i-boot' puh-BAWL'-sheh?

    smaller поменьше puh-M'EHN'-sheh

    longer подлиннее puhd-l'in-N'EH-yeh
    shorter покороче puh-kuh-RAW-cheh

I should like to see ——.
Я хотел (хотела) бы посмотреть ——.
yah khuh-T'EHL (khuh-T'EH-luh) by puhs-muh-TR'EHT'
——.

Show me ——.
Покажите мне ——.
puh-kuh-ZHY-t'eh mn'eh ——.

Give me ——.
Дайте мне ——.
DEYE-t'eh mn'eh ——.

How much is this (that)?
Сколько стоит это (то)?
SKAWL'-kuh STAW-yit EH-tuh (taw)?

Too much! I'll pay six rubles for it.
Слишком много! Я дал бы за это шесть рублей.
SL'EESH-kuhm MNAW-guh! yah dahl by zuh EH-tuh shehst'
roo-BL'EY.

Will you take it with you?
Вы это возьмёте с собой?
vy EH-tuh vuhz-M'AW-t'eh s suh-BOI?

Shall I send it?
Прислать вам это?
pr'is-LAHT' vahm EH-tuh?

Please wrap it up.
Пожалуйста заверните это.
puh-ZHAHL-stuh zuh-v'ir-N'EE-t'eh EH-tuh.

Please send it to the hotel.
Пожалуйста пошлите это в отель.
puh-ZHAHL-stuh puhsh-L'EE-t'eh EH-tuh vuh-T'EHL'.

I shall pay on delivery.
Я уплачу по доставке.
yah oo-pluh-CHOO puh duhs-TAHF-k'eh.

May I have my purchases sent to my ship?
Могут ли мои покупки быть доставлены на пароход?
MAW-goot l'i muh-YEE puh-KOOP-k'ee byt' duhs-TAHV-
l'i-ny nuh puh-ruh-KHAWT?

   to the airplane terminal
   на аэровокзал
   nuh uh-eh-ruh-vuhk-ZAHL

   to my home in the United States
   мне домой в Соединённые Штаты
   mn'eh duh-MOI fsuh-yi-d'i-N'AWN-ny-yeh SHTAH-ty

Please take my measurement.
Снимите с меня мерку пожалуйста.
sn'i-M'EE-t'eh sm'i-N'AH M'EHR-koo puh-ZHAHL-stuh.

Do you want to try it on?
Хотите примерить?
khuh-T'EE-t'eh pr'i-M'EH-r'it'?

It does not fit.
Это не подходит.
EH-tuh n'eh puht-KHAW-d'it.

The sleeves are too long (short, full, narrow).
Рукава слишком длинны (коротки, широки, тесны).
roo-kuh-VAH SL'EESH-kuhm dl'in-NY (kuh-ruht-K'EE, shy-
ruh-K'EE, t'is-NY).

Could I have a zipper put in?
Можно ли поставить тут зипер?
MAWZH-nuh l'i puhs-TAH-v'it' toot Z'EE-p'ir?

May I have a receipt?
Могу я получить расписку?
muh-GOO yah puh-loo-CHEET' ruhs-P'EES-koo?

116

I want one made of cotton.

Я хочу из (хлопчато)бумажной материи.

yah khuh-CHOO ees (khluhp-CHAH-tuh-)boo-MAHZH-noi
muh-T'EH-r'ee-i.

wool шерстяной материи shyr-st'uh-NOI muh-T'EH-r'ee-i

silk шёлка SH'AWL-kuh

rayon искуственного шёлка ees-KOOS-tv'in-nuh-vuh
SH'AWL-kuh

leather кожи KAW-zhy

lace кружева kroo-ZHEH-vuh

rubber резины r'i-Z'EE-ny

**I should like to buy the watch in the showcase (in the
window display).**

Я хотел (хотела) бы купить часы из выставочного ящика
(из витрины).

yah khuh-T'EHL (khuh-T'EH-luh) by koo-P'EET' chuh-SY
eez VYS-stuh-vuhch-nuh-vuh YAHSH-chy-kuh (eez v'i-
TR'EE-ny).

the bracelet браслет bruhs-L'EHT

the ring кольцо kuhl'-TSAW

the earrings серьги S'EHR'-g'ee

the necklace ожерелье uh-zhy-R'EHL'-yeh

the brooch (pin) брошку BRAWSH-koo

the sun glasses солнечные очки SAWL-n'ich-ny-yeh
uhch-K'EE

the alarm clock будильник boo-D'EEL'-n'ik

Do you repair watches?

Вы поправляете часы?

vy puh-pruh-VL'AH-yi-t'eh chuh-SY?

The spring of my wrist watch is broken.

В моих ручных часах лопнула пружинка.

vmuh-YIKH rooch-NYKH chuh-SAHKH LAWP-noo-luh
proo-ZHYN-kuh.

the crystal is broken
лопнуло стекло
LAWP-noo-luh st'ik-LAW

the strap is broken
лопнул ремешёк
LAWP-nool r'i-m'i-SH'AWK

This watch is fast (is slow).
Эти часы идут вперёд (отстают).
EH-t'ee chuh-SY ee-DOOT fp'i-R'AWT (uht-stuh-YOOT).

Can you put rubber heels on my shoes?
Вы можете поставить резиновые каблуки на мои ботинки?
vy MAW-zhy-t'eh puhs-TAH-v'it' r'i-Z'EE-nuh-vy-yeh kuh-
  bloo-K'EE nuh muh-YEE buh-T'EEN-k'ee?

Is it handmade (imported, domestic)?
Это ручной работы (импортированное, домашнего произ-
  водства)?
EH-tuh rooch-NOI ruh-BAW-ty (eem-puhr-T'EE-ruh-vuhn-
  nuh-yeh, duh-MAHSH-n'i-vuh pruh-iz-VAWT-stvuh)?

Can I return this article?
Могу ли я возвратить эту вещь?
muh-GOO l'i yah vuhz-vruh-T'EET' EH-too v'ehshch'?

How much can you spend?
Сколько вы могли бы истратить?
SKAWL'-kuh vy muhg-L'EE by ees-TRAH-t'it'?

How much is it worth?
Какая этому ценность?
kuh-KAH-yuh EH-tuh-moo TS'EHN-nuhst'?

I want a clothesbrush.
Я хотел (хотела) бы щётку для платья.
yah khuh-T'EHL (khuh-T'EH-luh) by SHCH'AWT-koo dl'uh
  PLAH-t'uh.

the perfume духи doo-KHEE

the cologne о-де-колон oh-duh-kuh-LAWN

the cold cream кольд-крем kuhl't-KR'EHM

the rouge румяна roo-M'AH-nuh

the lipstick губную помаду goob-NOO-yoo puh-MAH-
  doo

118

a toothbrush зубную щётку zoob-NOO-yoo SHCH'AWT-koo

the toothpaste зубную пасту zoob-NOO-yoo PAHS-too

a hairbrush щётку для волос SHCH'AWT-koo dl'uh vuh-LAWS

the hairpins шпильки SHP'EEL'-k'ee

the shoelaces шнурки для ботинок shnoor-K'EE dl'uh buh-T'EE-nuhk

a flatiron утюг oo-T'OOK

a corkscrew штопор SHTAW-puhr

a can opener открывалку для консервов uht-kry-VAHL-koo dl'uh kuhn-S'EHR-vuhf

the face powder пудру POO-droo

the nail polish лак для ногтей lahk dl'uh nuhk-T'EY

polish remover жидкость для удаления лака ZHYT-kuhst' dl'uh oo-duh-L'EH-n'i-yuh LAH-kuh

a comb гребёнку gr'i-B'AWN-koo

a hair net сетку для волос S'EHT-koo dl'uh vuh-LAWS

the soap мыло MY-luh

a razor бритву BR'EET-voo

the razor blades ножи для бритья nuh-ZHY dl'uh br'i-T'AH

a shaving brush кисточку для бритья K'EES-tuhch-koo dl'uh br'i-T'AH

the toilet paper клозетную бумагу kluh-Z'EHT-noo-yoo boo-MAH-goo

the shaving cream крем для бритья kr'ehm dl'uh br'i-T'AH

the hand lotion лосион для рук luh-s'i-AWN dl'uh rook

a box of chocolates коробку шоколада kuh-RAWP-koo shuh-kuh-LAH-duh

the safety pins английские булавки uhn-GL'EES-k'i-yeh boo-LAHF-k'ee

a suitcase чемодан chi-muh-DAHN

a deodorant дезодоратор d'i-zuh-duh-RAH-tuhr

I should like some camera film no. 5.

Я хотел (хотела) бы несколько катушек фильмов номер пять.
yah khuh-T'EHL (khuh-T'EH-luh) by N'EHS-kuhl'-kuh kuh-TOO-shehk F'EEL'-muhf NAW-m'ir p'aht'

a roll of color film катушку цветного фильма kuh-TOOSH-kco tsv'it-NAW-vuh F'EEL'-muh

some movie film несколько кино-фильмов N'EHS-kuhl'-kuh K'EE-nuh F'EEL'-muhf

a camera фотографический аппарат fuh-tuh-gruh-F'EE-chis-k'ee uh-puh-RAHT

How much does it cost to develop a roll?

Сколько стоит проявить катушку?
SKAWL'-kuh STAW-yit pruh-yuh-V'EET' kuh-TOOSH-koo?

I want one print of each (an enlargement).

Я хотел (хотела) бы по одному снимку (увеличению) от каждого.
yah khuh-T'EHL (khuh-T'EH-luh) by puh uhd-nuh-MOO SN'EEM-koo (oo-v'i-l'i-CHEH-n'i-yoo) uht KAHZH-duh-vuh.

When will it be ready?

Когда это будет готово?
kuhg-DAH EH-tuh BOO-d'it guh-TAW-vuh?

Can you repair this camera?

Можете ли вы поправить этот аппарат?
MAW-zhy-t'eh l'i vy puh-PRAH-v'it' EH-tuht uh-puh-RAHT?

˻ should like a package of cigarettes.

Я хотел (хотела) бы пакет папирос.
yah khuh-T'EHL (khuh-T'EH-luh) by puh-K'EHT puh-p'i-RAWS.

a box of cigars коробку сигар kuh-RAWP-koo s'i-GAHR

a tobacco pouch кисе. для табаку k'i-S'EHT dl'uh tuh-buh-KOO

a cigarette holder мундштук moont-SHTOOK

some pipe tobacco табаку для трубки tuh-buh-KOO dl'uh TROOP-k'ee

a silver cigarette case серебрянный портсигар s'i-R'EH-br'uhn-ny puhrt-ş'i-GAHR

a lighter зажигалку zuh-zhy-GAHL-koo

some flints кремень для зажигалки KR'EH-m'in' dl'uh zuh-zhy-GAHL-k'ee

some fluid жидкость для зажигалки ZHYT-kuhst' dl'uh zuh-zhy-GAHL-k'ee

some matches спички SP'EECH-k'ee

a pipe трубку TROOP-koo

Where is the liquor store?
Где винный магазин?
gd'eh V'EEN-ny muh-guh-Z'EEN?

I want a novel.
Я хотел (хотела) бы роман.
yah khuh-T'EHL (khuh-T'EH-luh) by ruh-MAHN.

a magazine журнал zhoor-NAHL

a newspaper газету guh-Z'EH-too

a pocket dictionary карманный словарь kuhr-MAHN-ny sluh-VAHR'

a guidebook путеводитель poo-t'i-vuh-D'EE-t'il'

a city map план города plahn GAW-ruh-duh

an automobile map автомобильную карту uhf-tuh-muh-B'EEL'-noo-yoo KAHR-too

the playing cards игральные карты ee-GRAHL'-ny-yeh KAHR-ty

a basket of fruit корзинку фруктов kuhr-Z'EEN-koo FROOK-tuhf

a fountain pen самопишущее перо suh-muh-P'EE-shoosh-chi-yeh p'i-RAW

the string верёвку v'i-R'AWF-koo

the wrapping paper обёрточную бумагу uh-B'AWR-tuhch-noo-yoo boo-MAH-goo

the carbon paper копировальную бумагу kuh-p'i-ruh-VAHL'-noo-yoo boo-MAH-goo

the picture post cards with views of the city открытки с видами города uhı-KRYT-k'ee sv'i-DAH-m'ee GAW-ruh-duh

We have none.
У нас нет.
oo nahs n'eht.

Anything else?
Что нибудь ещё?
SHTAW-n'i-boot' yish-CHAW?

Nothing else.
Больше ничего.
BAWL'-sheh n'i-chi-VAW.

That is all.
Это всё,
EH-tuh FS'AW

Here is your change (receipt).
Вот вам сдача (расписка).
vawt vahm SDAH-chuh (ruh-SP'EES-kuh).

Thank you very much.
Очень вам благодарен.
AW-chin' vahm bluh-guh-DAH-r'ehn.

At your service.
К вашим услугам.
KVAH-shym oo-SLOO-guhm.

Call again.
Заходите снова.
zuh-khuh-D'EE-t'eh SNAW-vuh

15
CABLE AND TELEPHONE

Where is the telegraph (telephone) office?
Где телеграфное (телефоное) отделение?
gd'eh t'i-l'i-GRAHF-nuh-yeh (t'i-l'i-FAW-nuh-yeh) uht-d'i-
L'EH-n'i-yeh?

What is the regular (night) rate per word to Vladivostok?
Какой нормальный (ночной) тариф за слово во Владивосток?
kuh-KOI nuhr-MAHL'-ny (nuhch-NOI) tuh-R'EEF zuh
SLAW-vuh vuh vluh-d'i-vuhs-TAWK?

When will it arrive?
Когда это придёт?
kuhg-DAH EH-tuh pr'i-D'AWT?

Where are the forms?
Где формуляры (бланки)?
gd'eh fuhr-moo-L'AH-ry (BLAHN-k'ee)?

Here is the address.
Вот адрес.
vawt AHD-r'ehs.

Where is the telephone (booth)?
Где телефон (телефонная будка)?
gd'eh t'i-l'i-FAWN (t'i-l'i-FAW-nuh-yuh BOOT-kuh)?

Do I need tokens for the phone?
Нужны ли жетоны для телефона?
noozh-NY l'i zhy-TAW-ny dl'uh t'i-l'i-FAW-nuh?

I want to make a local (long-distance) call to Taganrog.
Я хочу иметь местный (загородный) разговор с Таганрогом.
yah khuh-CHOO ee-M'EHT' M'EHST-ny (ZAH-guh-ruhd-ny)
ruhz-guh-VAWR stuh-guhn-RAW-guhm.

How much is the call to Arkhangelsk?
Сколько стоит разговор с Архангельском?
SKAWL'-kuh STAW-yit ruhz-guh-VAWR suhr-khuhn-
G'EHL'-skuhm?

At what time will he be back?

Когда он вернётся?

kuhg-DAH awn v'ir-N'AWT-suh?

He will be back at 5:30.

Он вернётся в пять тридцать.

awn v'ir-N'AWT-suh fp'aht' TR'EE-tsuht'.

Tell him Mr. Jones called.

Передайте, что ему звонил господин Джонс.

p'i-r'i-DEYE-t'eh, shtaw yi-MOO zvuh-N'EEL guhs-puh-D'EEN dzhohns.

Have him call me.

Пусть он позвонит мне.

poost' awn puhz-vuh-N'EET mn'eh.

What is your number?

Как ваш номер телефона?

kahk vahsh NAW-m'ir t'i-l'i-FAW-nuh?

Mr. Kuznetsov called; he left no message, but he'll call again at 5.

Звонил гражданин Кузнецов; он ничего не передавал, но он позвонит снова в пять часов.

zvuh-N'EEL gruhzh-duh-N'EEN kooz-n'i-TSAWF; awn n'i-chi-VAW n'eh p'i-r'i-duh-VAHL, nuh awn puhz-vuh-N'EET SNAW-vuh fp'aht' chuh-SAWF.

You can reach him at this number.

Вы можете получить его по этому номеру.

vy MAW-zhy-t'eh puh-loo-CHEET' yi-VAW puh EH-tuh-moo NAW-m'i-roo.

You have the wrong number.

У вас ошибочный номер.

оо vahs uh-SHY-buhch-ny NAW-m'ir.

Operator, you gave me the wrong number.

Оператор, вы дали мне ошибочный номер.

uh-p'i-RAH-tuhr, vy DAH-l'ee mn'eh uh-SHY-buhch-ny NAW-m'ir.

Hello! Who is speaking?

Алло! Кто говорит?

ahl-LAW! khtaw guh-vuh-R'EET?

This is Mr. (Mrs.) Ivanovsky.

Это гражданин Ивановский (гражданка Ивановская).

EH-tuh gruhzh-duh-N'EEN ee-vuh-NAWF-sk'ee (gruhzh-DAHN-kuh ee-vuh-NAWF-skuh-vuh).

124

Operator, get me number 5-64-78.
Оператор, дайте мне номер пять-шестьдесят четыре-семь-
    десят восемь.
uh-p'i-RAH-tuhr, DEYE-t'eh mn'eh NAW-m'ir p'aht' shyst'-
    d'i-S'AHT chi-TY-r'eh S'EHM'-d'i-s'uht VAW-s'im'.

You are connected.
Вы имеете связь.
vy ee-M'EH-yi-t'eh zv'ahs'.

They don't answer.
Нет ответа.
n'eht uht-V'EH-tuh.

The line is busy.
Линия занята.
L'EE-n'i-yuh zuh-n'uh-TAH.

The operator will call you.
Оператор вас позовёт.
uh-p'i-RAH-tuhr vahs puh-zuh-V'AWT.

Whom do you want to speak to?
С кем вы хотите говорить?
sk'ehm vy khuh-T'EE-t'eh guh-vuh-R'EET'?

I should like to speak to Mr. Ivanovsky.
Я хотел (хотела) бы поговорить с господином Ивановским.
yah khuh-T'EHL (khuh-T'EH-luh) by puh-guh-vuh-R'EET'
    sguhs-puh-D'EE-nuhm ee-vuh-NAWF-sk'im.

He is not here; may I take a message?
Его здесь нет; могу ли я что нибудь передать ему?
yi-VAW zd'ehs' n'eht; muh-GOO l'i yah SHTAW-n'i-boot'
    p'i-r'i-DAHT' yi-MOO?

Hold the wire.
Не вешайте трубку.
n'eh V'EH-sheye-t'eh TROOP-koo.

16

TRAVEL BY TAXI OR OTHER HIRED CONVEYANCE

Please wait for me.
Пожалуйста подождите меня.
puh-ZHAHL-stuh puh-duhzh-D'EE-t'eh m'i-N'AH.

I'm not allowed to wait here.
Мне не разрешается здесь ждать.
mn'eh n'i ruhz-r'i-SHAH-yit-suh zd'ehs' zhdaht'.

Drive more slowly (faster, more carefully).
Поезжайте медленнее (скорее, более осторожно).
puh-yiz-ZHEYE-t'eh M'EHD-l'in-n'i-yeh (skuh-R'EH-yeh,
   BAW-l'i-yeh uhs-tuh-RAWZH-nuh).

That's not the price we agreed upon.
Это не та цена, на которую мы согласились.
EH-tuh n'i tuh tsy-NAH, nuh kuh-TAW-roo-yoo my suh-gluh-
   S'EE-l'ees'.

That's not the price on the meter.
Это не цена на счётчике.
Eh-tuh n'i ts'i-NAH nuh SCHAWT-chi-k'eh.

Driver (coachman), what is your rate to the Kremlin?
Шофёр (извощик), сколько вы возьмёте до Кремля?
shuh-F'AWR (eez-VAWSH-chik), SKAWL'-kuh vy vuhz'-
   M'AW-t'eh duh kr'im-L'AH?

What is the hourly (daily) rate?
Сколько стоит по часам (за день)?
SKAWL'-kuh STAW-yit puh chuh-SAHM (ZAH-d'ehn')?

The luggage is extra.
За багаж отдельно.
zuh buh-GASH uht-D'EHL'-nuh.

Take the shortest way.
Поезжайте кратчайшим путём.
puh-yiz-ZHEYE-t'eh kruht-CHEYE-şhym poo-T'AWM.

Where to?
Куда?
koo-DAH?

Let's take a horse carriage and go on an excursion.
Давайте возьмём экипаж и поедем в экскурсию.
duh-VEYE-t'eh vuz'-M'AWM eh-k'i-PAHSH ee puh-YEH-
d'im vehk-SKOOR-s'yoo.

Drive around the city.
Поезжайте вокруг города.
puh-yiz-ZHEYE-t'eh vuh-KROOK GAW-ruh-duh.

   through the shopping (theater) district
   Через торговую (театральную) часть
   CHEH-r'is tuhr-GAW-voo-yoo (t'yuh-TRAHL'-noo-yoo)
   chahst'

Stop here; I want to get out.
Остановитесь тут; я хочу выйти.
uhs-tuh-nuh-V'EE-t'is' toot; yah khuh-CHOO VY-t'ee.

Show me the points of interest.
Покажите мне интересные места (достопримечательности).
puh-kuh-ZHY-t'eh mn'eh een-t'i-R'EHS-ny-eh m'is-TAH
   (duhs-tuh-pr'i-m'i-CHAH-t'il'-nuhs-t'ee).

17

DRIVING YOUR OWN CAR

There's something wrong with the bearing.
Что-то не в порядке с подшипниками.
HTAW-tuh n'i fpuh-R'AHT-k'eh spuht-SHYP-n'i-kuh-m'ee.

with the exhaust
с выхлопной трубой
zvykh-luhp-NOI troo-BOI

with the gears
с передачей
sp'i-r'i-DAH-chey

with the gear shift
с коробкой скоростей
skuh-RAWP-koi skuh-ruhs-T'EY

with the gas tank
с резервуаром для горючего бензина (*or* с бензиновым баком)
sr'i-z'ir-voo-AH-ruhm dl'uh guh-R'OO-chi-vuh b'in-Z'EE-nuh (zb'in-Z'EE-nuh-vym BAH-kuhm)

with the radiator
в радиаторе
vruh-d'i-AH-tuh-r'eh

with the starter
в стартере
FSTAHR-t'i-r'eh

with the steering wheel
с рулём
sroo-L'AWM

with the trunk
в багажном отделении
vbuh-GAHZH-nuhm uht-d'i-L'EH-n'ee-i

with the wheel
с колесом
skuh-l'i-SAWM

128

with the ignition
в зажигании
vzuh-zhy-GAH-n'ee-i

with the hood
с покрышкой (*or* с капотом)
spuh-KRYSH-koi (skuh-PAW-tuhm)

I have a breakdown.
У меня поломка.
oo m'i-N'AH puh-LAWM-kuh.

Can you tow me?
Можете ли взять меня на буксир?
MAW-zhy-t'eh l'i vz'aht' m'i-N'AH nuh book-S'EER?

How much a liter?
Сколько стоит литр?
SKAWL'-kuh STAW-yit l'eetr?

Fill her up!
Наполните!
nuh-PAWL-n'i-t'eh!

Give me thirty liters, please.
Дайте пожалуйста тридцать литров.
DEYE-t'eh puh-ZHAHL-stuh TR'EE-tsuht' L'EE-truhf.

Do I need oil (water, air)?
Нужно ли масла (воды, подкачать шины)?
NOOZH-nuh l'i MAHS-luh (vuh-DY, puht-kuh-CHAHT' SHY-ny)?

Do you have a road map?
Есть ли у вас дорожная карта?
YEHST'-l'i oo vahs duh-RAWZH-nuh-yuh KAHR-tuh?

Is there a good hotel (restaurant) in Pinsk?
Есть ли хороший отель (ресторан) в Пинске?
YEHST'-li khuh-RAW-shy uh-T'EHL' (r'is-tuh-RAHN) FP'EEN-sk'eh?

Is the auto highway good?
Хороша ли автострада?
khuh-ruh-SHAH l'i uhf-tuh-STRAH-duh?

Please check the tires.
Проверьте пожалуйста шины.
pruh-V'EHR'-t'eh puh-ZHAHL-stuh SHY-ny.

the oil
масло
MAHS-luh

the water
воду
VAW-doo

the battery
батарею
buh-tuh-R'EH-yoo

the spark plugs
свечи
ZV'EH-chee

How far is the next gas station?
Как далеко до следующей бензинной станции?
kahk duh-l'i-KAW duh SL'EH-doo-yoosh-chey b'in-Z'EEN-noi STAHN-tsee-i?

Go four blocks and turn left.
Поезжайте четыре квартала и поверните налево.
puh-yiz-ZHEYE-t'eh chi-TY-r'eh kvuhr-TAH-luh ee puh-v'ir-N'EE-t'eh nuh-L'EH-vuh.

Is this the way to Rostov-na-Donu?
Эта дорога в Ростов-на-Дону?
EH-tuh duh-RAW-guh vruhs-TAWF-nuh-duh-NOO?

Turn left after you pass the bridge, then straight.
Поверните налево после того, как проедете мост, затем поезжайте прямо.
puh-v'ir-N'EE-t'eh nuh-L'EH-vuh PAWS-l'eh tuh-VAW, kahk pruh-YEH-d'i-t'eh mawst, zuh-T'EHM puh-yiz-ZHEYE-t'eh PR'AH-muh.

Which is the road to Orel?
Которая дорога в Орёл?
kuh-TAW-ruh-yuh duh-RAW-guh vuh-R'AWL?

You turn right at the next corner (at the crossroad, at the stop light).

Поверните направо на следующем углу (на перекрёстке, у светового сигнала).

puh-v'ir-N'EE-t'eh nuh-PRAH-vuh nuh SL'EH-doo-yoosh-chim oo-GLOO (nuh p'i-r'i-KR'AWST-k'eh, oo sv'eh-tuh-VAW-vuh s'ig-NAH-luh).

Is the road good?

Хороша ли дорога?

khuh-ruh-SHAH l'i duh-RAW-guh?

Where is the garage?

Где гараж?

gd'eh guh-RAHSH?

May I leave my car here?

Могу ли я оставить мой автомобиль здесь?

muh-GOO l'i yah uhs-TAH-v'it' moi uhf-tuh-muh-B'EEL' zd'ehs'?

Where may I park?

Где я могу поставить машину?

gd'eh yah muh-GOO puhs-TAH-v'it' muh-SHY-noo?

Will you change the oil?

Перемените масло.

p'i-r'i-m'i-N'EE-t'eh MAHS-luh.

Light, medium or heavy?

Лёгкое, среднее или тяжёлое?

LYAWKH-kuh-yeh, SR'EHD-n'i-yeh EE-l'ee t'uh-ZHAW-luh-yeh?

I have a flat; can you change it (fix it)?

У меня спустила шина; можете ли вы переменить её (привести в порядок)?

oo m'i-N'AH spoos-T'EE-luh SHY-nuh; MAW-zhy-t'eh l'i vy p'i-r'i-m'i-N'EET' yi-YAW (pr'i-v'is-T'EE fpuh-R'AH-duhk)?

Help me jack up the car.

Помогите мне поднять машину.

puh-muh-G'EE-t'eh mn'eh puhd-N'AHT' muh-SHY-noo.

Have you a spare?

Есть ли у вас запасная шина?

YEHST'-l'i oo vahs zuh-puhs-NAH-yuh SHY-nuh?

131

Is there a mechanic here?
Есть ли тут механик?
YEHST'-l'i toot m'i-KHAH-n'ik?

How much are the repairs?
Сколько за починку?
SKAWL'-kuh zuh puh-CHEEN-koo?

Can you fix it?
Можете ли вы это поправить?
MAW-zhy-t'eh l'i vy EH-tuh puh-PRAH-v'it'?

I can fix it temporarily.
Я могу это починить временно.
yah muh-GOO EH-tuh puh-chi-N'EET' VR'EH-m'in-nuh.

How long will it take?
Сколько времени на это пойдёт?
SKAWL'kuh VR'EH-m'i-n'ee nuh EH-tuh poi-D'AWT?

I can't do it today.
Я не могу это сделать сегодня.
yah n'i muh-GOO EH-tuh ZD'EH-luht' s'i-VAWD-n'uh.

I have to send for parts.
Я должен (должна) послать за запасными частями.
yah DAWL-zhyn (duhl-ZHNAH) puhs-LAHT' zuh zuh-PAHS-
ny-m'ee chus-T'AH-m'ee.

I need a cable.
Мне нужен провод.
mn'eh NOO-zhyn PRAW-vuht.

   a screwdriver
   отвёртка
   uht-V'AWRT-kuh

I need a fender.
Мне нужно крыло.
mn'eh NOOZH-nuh kry-LAW.

   a headlight
   фар
   fahr

I need a pair of pliers.
Мне нужны плоскогубцы.
mn'eh noozh-NY pluhs-kuh-GOOP-tsy.

I need a bulb.
Мне нужна лампочка.
mn'eh noozh-NAH LAHM-puhch-kuh.

a door handle
дверная ручка
dv'ir-NAH-yuh ROOCH-kuh

a nut
гайка
GEYE-kuh

a fuel pump
бензиновая помпа
b'in-Z'EE-nuh-vuh-yuh PAWM-puh

an inner tube
камера
KAH-m'i-ruh

a tail light
задняя сигнальная лампочка
ZAHD-n'uh-yuh s'ig-NAHL'-nuh-yuh LAHM-puhch-kuh

a fan
вентилятор
v'in-t'i-L'AH-tuhr

a fan belt
ремень для вентилятора
r'i-M'EHN' dl'uh v'in-t'i-L'AH-tuh-ruh

a bolt
болт
bawlt

a horn
кляксон
kl'ahk-SAWN

a jack
домкрат
duhm-KRAHT

a wrench
гаечный ключ
GAH-yich-ny kl'ooch

a hammer
молоток
muh-luh-TAWK

133

This car doesn't run well (doesn't go).

Эта машина плохо идёт (не идёт).

EH-tuh muh-SHY-nuh PLAW-khuh ee-D'AWT (n'i ee-D'AWT).

The battery is dead.

Батарея не действует.

bu-tuh-R'EH-yuh n'i D'EYS-tvoo-yit.

There is a grinding (noise, rattle, squeak).

Там что-то скребёт (шумит, трещит, скрипит).

tahm SHTAW-tuh skr'i-B'AWT (shoo-M'EET, tr'ish-CHEET, skr'i-P'EET).

The engine overheats (stalls).

Машина перегревается (останавливается).

muh-SHY-nuh p'i-r'i-gr'i-VAH-yit-suh (uhs-tuh-NAHV-l'i-vuh-yit-suh).

Please grease the car.

Подмажьте пожалуйста машину.

pùhd-MAHSH'-t'eh puh-ZHAHL-stuh muh-SHY-noo.

Tighten the brakes.

Подтяните тормоза.

puht-t'uh-N'EE-t'eh tuhr-muh-ZAH.

Adjust the carburetor (the clutch).

Отрегулируйте карбюратор (коробку скоростей *or* сцепление).

uht-r'i-goo-L'EE-rooy-t'eh kuhr-b'oo-RAH-tuhr (kuh-RAWP-koo skuh-ruhs-T'EY, stsy-PL'EH-n'i-yeh).

Wash the car.

Помойте машину.

puh-MOI-t'eh muh-SHY-noo.

Put water in the battery, radiator.

Налейте воды в батарею, в радиатор.

nuh-L'EY-t'eh vuh-DY vbuh-tuh-R'EH-yoo, vruh-d'i-AH-tuhr.

Where is the key?

Где ключ?

gd'eh kl'ooch?

18

TRAVEL BY TRAIN OR PLANE

Which is the train (plane) to Sverdlovsk?
Который поезд (самолёт) в Свердловск?
kuh-TAW-ry   PAW-yehst   (suh-muh-L'AWT)   vsv'ehrt-
   LAWFSK?

Track number six.
Перон номер шесть.
p'i-RAWN NAW-m'ir shehst'.

Runway number five.
Дорожка номер пять.
duh-RAWSH-kuh NAW-m'ir p'aht'.

Does this train stop at Sevastopol?
Останавливается ли этот поезд в Севастополе?
uhs-tuh-NAHV-l'i-vuh-yit-suh l'i EH-tuht PAW-yehst îs'i-
   vuhs-TAW-puh-l'eh?

How long does it stop?
Как долго остановка?
kahk DAWL-guh uhs-tuh-NAWF-kuh?

**Please put my baggage in my compartment (on the train,
   on the plane).**
Отнесите пожалуйста мой багаж в моё купэ (в поезд, на
   самолёт).
uht-n'i-S'EE-t'eh puh-ZHAHL-stuh moi buh-GAHSH vmuh-
   YAW koo-PEH (FPAW-yehst, nuh suh-muh-L'AWT).

Will you put this bag in the rack?
Положите этот чемодан в сетку.
puh-luh-ZHY-t'eh EH-tuht chi-muh-DAHN FS'EHT-koo.

Is this seat taken?
Это место занято?
EH-tuh M'EHS-tuh ZAH-n'uh-tuh?

No, it's free.
Нет, оно свободно.
n'eht, uh-NAW zvuh-BAWD-nuh.

On what track does the Moscow train leave?
С какого перона отходит поезд в Москву?
skuh-KAW-vuh p'i-RAW-nuh uht-KHAW-d'it PAW-yehst
  vmuhsk-VOO?

Where are the first- (second-) class cars?
Где вагоны первого (второго) класса?
gd'eh vuh-GAW-ny P'EHR-vuh-vuh (ftuh-RAW-vuh) KLAH-
  suh?

Ahead (behind).
Впереди (сзади).
fp'i-r'i-D'EE (ZZAH-d'•).

When do we arrive at Pyatigorsk?
Когда мы прибываем в Пятигорск?
kuhg-DAH my pr'i-by-VAH-yim fp'uh-t'i-GAWRSK?

At 5:10.
В пять десять.
fp'aht' D'EH-s'uht'.

In half an hour.
Через полчаса.
CHEH-r'is puhl-chuh-SAH.

Is the train on time?
Приходит ли поезд во время?
pr'i-KHAW-d'it l'i PAW-yehst VAW-vr'i-m'uh?

We are fifteen minutes late.
Мы опаздываем на пятнадцать минут.
my uh-PAHZ-dy-vuh-yim nuh p'uht-NAH-tsuht' m'i-NOOT.

Why are we stopping?
Почему мы стоим?
puh-chi-MOO my stuh-YEEM?

What is the matter?
В чём дело?
fchawm D'EH-luh?

Where are you going?
Куда вы едете? (by conveyance) идёте? (on foot or by boat)
koo-DAH vy YEH-d'i-t'eh (ee-D'AW-t'eh)?

I am going by train (plane) to Irkutsk.
Я еду поездом (я лечу на самолёте) в Иркутск.
yah YEH-doo PAW-yiz-duhm (yah L'EH-choo nuh suh-muh-
  L'AW-t'eh) v'ir-KOOTSK.

All aboard!
Садитесь! (*or* Третий звонок!)
suh-D'EE-t'ehs'! (TR'EH-t'ee zvuh-NAWK!)

All visitors off the platform!
Все провожающие должны очистить платформу!
fs'eh pruh-vuh-ZHAH-yoosh-chi-yeh DAWL-zhny uh-CHEES-t'it' pluht-FAWR-moo!

Where is the dining car?
Где вагон-ресторан?
gd'eh vuh-GAWN-r'is-tuh-RAHN?

Five cars ahead (behind).
Пять вагонов вперёд (назад).
p'aht' vuh-GAW-nuhf fp'i'R'AWT (nuh-ZAHT).

Where is the smoker?
Где вагон для курящих?
gd'eh vuh-GAWN dl'uh koo-R'AHSH-chikh?

Last car on the train.
Последний вагон.
puhs-L'EHD-n'ee vuh-GAWN.

Is there a sleeping car on this train?
Есть ли в этом поезде спальный вагон?
YEHST'-l'i VEH-tuhm PAW-yiz-d'eh SPAHL'-ny vuh-GAWN?

First call for dinner (breakfast, lunch).
Первый звонок на о   ; (утренний чай, завтрак).
P'EHR-vy zvuh-NAWK nuh uh-B'EHT (OO-tr'in-n'ee cheye, ZAHF-truhk).

Is there time to get something to eat?
Есть ли время что нибудь съесть?
YEHST'-l'i VR'EH-m'ah SHTAW-n'i-boot' syehst'?

At the next stop you can get a sandwich or a lunch basket.
На следующей остановке вы можете получить бутерброд или завтрак в корзинке.
nuh SL'EH-doo-yoosh-chey uh-stuh-NAWF-k'eh vy MAW-zhy-t'eh puh-loo-CHEET' boo-t'ir-BRAWT EE-l'ee ZAHF-truhk fkuhr-Z'EEN-k'eh.

I have a reserved seat (compartment).
У меня резервированное место (купэ).
oo m'i-N'AH r'i-z'ir-V'EE-ruh-vuhn-nuh-yeh M'EHS-tuh (koo-PEH).

137

Where is the airlines office?

Где контора аэролинии?

gd'eh kuhn-TAW-ruh uh-eh-ruh-L'EE-n'ee?

Is there motor service to the airport?

Есть ли автомобильное сообщение с аэродромом?

YEHST'-l'i uhf-tuh-muh-B'EEL'-nuh-yeh suh-uhpsh-CHEH-
   n'i-yeh suh-eh-ruh-DRAW-muhm?

Are you the conductor?

Вы кондуктор?

vy kuhn-DOOK-tuhr?

No, I'm the Pullman porter.

Нет, я проводник шульманского вагона.

n'eht, yah pruh-vuhd-N'EEK POOL'-muhn-skuh-vuh vuh-
   GAW-nuh.

Where is the stewardess (hostess)?

Где стюардесса (проводница)?

gd'eh st'oo-uhr-D'EHS-suh (pruh-vuhd-N'EE-tsuh)?

I am the stewardess.

Я стюардесса.

yah st'oo-uhr-D'EHS-suh.

Is this an express or a local train?

Этот поезд скорый или пассажирский?

EH-tuht PAW-yist SKAW-ry EE-l'ee puh-suh-ZHYR-sk'ee?

Wait for me at the gate.

Ждите меня у входа.

ZHD'EE-t'eh m'i-N'AH oo FKHAW-duh.

May I open the window?

Могу ли я открыть окно?

muh-GOO l'i yah uht-KRYT' uhk-NAW?

Please close the window.

Закройте пожалуйста окно.

zuh-KROI-t'eh puh-ZHAHL-stuh uhk-NAW.

There is a draft.

Там сквозняк.

tahm skvuhz-N'AHK.

Please call me at seven.

Разбудите меня пожалуйста в семь.

ruhz-boo-D'EE-t'eh m'i-N'AH puh-ZHAHL-stuh fs'ehm'.

Shall I prepare your berth?
Сделать вам койку?
ZD'EH-luht' vahm KOI-koo?

Please prepare it early.
Сделайте пожалуйста пораньше.
ZD'EH-leye-t'eh puh-ZHAHL-stuh puh-RAHN'-sheh.

Here is the railroad station (airport).
Тут железнодорожная станция (*or* вокзал) (аэропорт).
toot zhy-l'iz-nuh-duh-RAWZH-nuh-yuh STAHN-tsyuh (vuhg-
    ZAHL) (uh-eh-ruh-PAWRT).

19

TRAVEL BY BUS OR STREETCAR

Where can I get a bus to Nevsky Prospekt?
Где остановка автобуса на Невском Проспекте?
gd'eh uhs-tuh-NAWF-kuh uhf-TAW-boo-suh nuh N'EHF-
skuhm pruhs-P'EHK-t'eh?

Driver, will you please tell me where to get off?
Шофёр, скажите мне пожалуйста, где мне выходить?
shuh-F'AWR, skuh-ZHY-t'eh mn'eh puh-ZHAHL-stuh, gd'eh
mn'eh vy-khuh-D'EET'?

Get off at the next stop (next block, corner).
Сойдите на следующей остановке (следующем квартале,
углу)
soi-D'EE-t'eh nuh SL'EH-doo-yoosh-chey uhs-tuh-NAWF-
k'eh (SL'EH-doo-yoosh-chim gvuhr-TAH-l'eh, oo-GLOO).

Get off here.
Выходите здесь.
vy-khuh-D'EE-t'eh zd'ehs'.

Do I have to transfer?
Должен (должна) ли я пересесть?
DAWL-zhyn (duhl-ZHNAH) l'i yah p'i-r'i-S'EHST'?

Yes, take the number-five bus.
Да, возьмите автобус номер пять.
dah, vuhz'-M'EE-t'eh uhf-TAW-boos NAW-m'ir p'aht'.

Do I have to buy a token?
Должен (должна) ли я купить жетон?
DAWL-zhyn (duhl-ZHNAH) l'i yah koo-P'EET' zhy-TAWN?

When does this bus return from Yalta?
Когда этот автобус возвращается из Ялты?
kuhg-DAH EH-tuht uhf-TAW-boos vuhz-vruhsh-CHAH-yit-
suh eez YAHL-ty?

Let me off at the Academy of Sciences.
Дайте мне сойти у Академии Наук.
DEYE-t'eh mn'eh soi-T'EE oo uh-kuh-D'EH-m'ee nuh-OOK.

I want to go to Lenin's Tomb.

Я хочу проехать к Мавзолею Ленина.

yah khuh-CHOO pruh-YEH-khuht' kmuhv-zuh-L'EH-yoo
L'EH-n'i-nuh.

Is it far from here?

Далеко ли это отсюда?

duh-l'i-KAW l'i EH-tuh uht-S'OO-duh?

Does this bus (streetcar) go to Children's Village?

Идёт ли этот автобус (трамвай) в Детскую Деревню?

ee-D'AWT l'i EH-tuht uhf-TAW-boos (truhm-VEYE)
VD'EHT-skoo-yoo d'i-R'EHV-n'oo?

Yes, wait at the bus (car) stop.

Да. подождите на остановке автобуса (трамвая).

dah, puh-duhzh-D'EE-t'eh nuh uhs-tuh-NAWF-k'eh uhf-
TAW-boo-suh (truhm-VAH-yuh).

How much is the fare to Red Square?

Сколько стоит проезд до Красной Площади?

SKAWL'-kuh STAW-yit pruh-YEHST duh KRAHS-noi
PLAWSH-chuh-d'ee?

I feel seasick.

Я болен (больна) морской болезнью.

yah BAW-l'ehn (buhl'-NAH) muhr-SKOI buh-L'EHZ-n'yoo.

Have you a remedy for seasickness?

Есть ли у вас средство от морской болезни?

YEHST'-l'i oo vahs SR'EHT-stvuh uht muhr-SKOI buh-L'EHZ-n'ee?

I am going to my stateroom.

Я иду в мою каюту.

yah ee-DOO vmuh-YOO kuh-YOO-too.

Take me to my stateroom.

Отведите меня в мою каюту.

uht-v'i-D'EE-t'eh m'i-N'AH vmuh-YOO kuh-YOO-too.

I'm going on deck.

Я иду на палубу.

yah ee-DOO nuh PAH-loo-boo.

Is there a swimming pool on board?

Есть ли на пароходе бассейн для плавания?

YEHST'-l'i nuh puh-ruh-KHAW-d'eh buhs-S'EYN dl'uh PLAH-vuh-n'yuh?

I should like to sit at the captain's (doctor's, first mate's) table.

Я хотел (хотела) бы сидеть за столом капитана (доктора, первого помощника капитана).

yah khuh-T'EHL (khuh-T'EH-luh) by s'i-D'EHT' zuh stuh-LAWM kuh-p'i-TAH-nuh (DAWK-tuh-ruh, P'EHR-vuh-vuh puh-MAWSHCH-n'i-kuh kuh-p'i-TAH-nuh).

Where are you landing?

Где вы выходите?

gd'eh vy vy-KHAW-d'i-t'eh?

I am landing at Riga.

Я выхожу в Риге.

yah vy-khuh-ZHOO VR'EE-g'eh.

The ship sails from the company's pier.
Пароход отходит от пристани общества.
puh-ruh-KHAWT uht-KHAW-d'it uht PR'EE-stuh-n'ee AWP-shchist-vuh.

I should like to speak to the captain (purser, deck steward).
Я хотел (хотела) бы поговорить с капитаном (с экономом с слугой).
yah khuh-T'EHL (khuh-T'EH-luh) by puh-guh-vuh-R'EET' skuh-p'i-TAH-nuhm (seh-kuh-NAW-muhm, sloo-GOI).

When does the next ship leave?
Когда отходит следующий пароход?
kuhg-DAH uht-KHAW-d'it SL'EH-doo-yoosh-chee puh-ruh-KHAWT?

At 5:45 p.m.
В пять сорок пять дня (*or* в семнадцать сорок пять).
fp'aht' SAW-ruhk 'p'aht' dn'ah (fs'im-NAH-tsuht' SAW-ruhk p'aht').

May visitors go on board?
Могут ли посетители войти на пароход?
MAW-goot l'i puh-s'i-T'EE-t'i-l'ee voi-T'EE nuh puh-ruh-KHAWT?

I want to rent a deck chair.
Я хочу нанять платное кресло.
yah khuh-CHOO nuh-N'AHT' PLAHT-nuh-yeh KR'EHS-luh.

At what time are meals served?
В котором часу подается еда?
fkuh-TAW-ruhm chuh-SOO puh-duh-YEHT-suh yi-DAH?

Breakfast seven to nine.
Утренний чай от семи до девяти.
OO-tr'in-n'ee cheye uht s'i-M'EE duh d'i-v'uh-T'EE.

Lunch twelve to two.
Завтрак от двенадцати до двух.
ZAHF-truhk uht dv'i-NAH-tsuh-t'ee duh dvookh.

Dinner six to eight.
Обед от шести до девяти.
uh-B'EHT uht shys-T'EE duh d'i-v'uh-T'EE.

Where is the dining salon (lounge)?
Где столовая (кают-кампания)?
gd'eh stuh-LAW-vuh-yuh (kuh-YOOT-kuhm-PAH-n'yuh)?

On Deck B.

На палубе Б.

nuh PAH-loo-b'eh b'eh.

Where are the lifeboats (life preservers)?

Где спасательные лодки (спасательная одежда)?

gd'eh spuh-SAH-t'il'-ny-yeh LAWT-k'ee (spuh-SAH-t'il'-nuh-
   yuh uh-D'EHZH-duh)?

21

TICKETS

I want a ticket to Kirov.
Я хочу билет в Киров
yah khuh-CHOO b'i-L'EHT FK'EE-ruhf.

one-way
в один конец
vuh-D'EEN kuh-N'EHTS

round-trip
туда и обратно
too-DAH ee uh-BRAHT-nuh

first, second, third class
первого, второго, третьего класса
P'EHR-vuh-vuh, ftuh-RAW-vuh, TR'EH-t'i-vuh KLAH-suh

I want a timetable.
Я хочу расписание.
yah khuh-CHOO ruhs-p'i-SAH-n'yeh.

a reserved seat
плацкартное место
pluhts-KAHRT-nuh-yeh M'EHS-tuh

a seat in the middle of the coach
место в середине вагона
M'EHS-tuh fs'i-r'i-D'EE-n'eh vuh-GAW-nuh

an upper berth
верхнюю койку
V'EHRKH-n'oo-yoo KOI-koo

a lower berth
нижнюю койку
N'EEZH-n'oo-yoo KOI-koo

a compartment
купэ
koo-PEH

travel insurance
страховой полис
struh-khuh-VOI PAW-l'is

Where is the ticket office?
Где билетная касса?
gd'eh b'i-L'EHT-nuh-yuh KAHS-suh?

the information desk
справочное бюро
SPRAH-vuhch-nuh-yeh b'oo-RAW

the stationmaster
начальник станции
nuh-CHAHL'-n'ik STAHN-tsee

the waiting room
зал для ожидания
zahl dl'uh uh-zhy-DAH-n'i-yuh

the men's room
мужская уборная
moosh-SKAH-yuh oo-BAWR-nuh-yuh

the ladies' room
дамская уборная
DAHM-skuh-yuh oo-BAWR-nuh-yuh

Where can I buy a ticket?
Где могу я купить билет?
gd'eh muh-GOO yah koo-P'EET' b'i-L'EHT?

At the ticket window on the right.
В кассе направо.
FKAHS-s'eh nuh-PRAH-vuh.

Where do you want to go?
Куда вы хотите ехать?
koo-DAH vy khuh-T'EE-t'eh YEH-khuht'?

I want to go to Moscow.
Я хочу поехать в Москву.
yah khuh-CHOO puh-YEH-khuht' vmuhsk-VOO.

Where is the railroad station?
Где вокзал?
gd'eh vuhg-ZAHL?

How can I reach it from here?
Как я могу отсюда проехать туда?
kahk yah muh-GOO uht-S'OO-duh pruh-YEH-khuht' too-
DAH?

146

Where can I get the train to Kazan?

Где поезд на Казань?

gd'eh PAW-yehst nuh kuh-ZAHN'?

I want to take the 9:30 train.

Я хочу ехать с поездом в девять тридцать.

yah khuh-CHOO YEH-khuht' SPAW-yehz-duhm VD'EH-
v'uht' TR'EE-tsuht'.

How much is a ticket to Odessa?

Сколько стоит билет до Одессы?

SKAWL'kuh STAW-yit b'i-L'EHT duh uh-D'EHS-sy?

How long is the ticket good for?

На какое время действителен билет?

nuh kuh-KAW-yeh VR'EH-m'uh d'evst-V'EE-t'i-l'ehn b'i-
L'EHT?

Ten days.

Десять дней.

D'EH-s'uht' dn'ey.

I want to change my reservation from 10:30 to 4:30.

Я хочу переменить время отъезда с десяти тридцати на
четыре тридцать.

yah khuh-CHOO p'i-r'i-m'i-N'EET' VR'EH-m'uh uht-YEHZ-
duh zd'i-s'uh-T'EE TR'EE-tsuh-t'ee nuh chi-TY-r'eh TR'EE-
tsuht'.

At what time does the train for Stalingrad leave?

Когда идёт поезд в Сталинград?

kuhg-DAH ee-D'AWT PAW-yehst fstuh-l'in-GRAHT?

It leaves at 6 p.m.

Он уходит (or идёт) в шесть часов вечера.

awn oo-KHAW-d'it (ee-D'AWT) fshehst' chu-SAWF V'EH-
chi-ruh.

It leaves in twenty minutes.

Он уходит (or идёт) через двадцать минут.

awn oo-KHAW-d'it (ee-D'AWT) CHEH-r'is DVAH-tsuht'
m'i-NOOT.

I want to go by way of Dniepropetrovsk.

Я хочу ехать через Днепропетровск.

yah khuh-CHOO YEH-khuht' CHEH-r'is dn'eh-pruh-p'i-
TRAWFSK.

May I stop over at Kiev?
Могу ли я остановиться в Киеве?
muh-GOO l'i yah uh-stuh-nuh-V'EET'-suh FK'EE-yeh-v'eh?

Do I have to change trains?
Имею ли я пересадку?
ee-M'EH-yoo l'i yah p'i-r'i-SAHT-koo?

Yes, change at Smolensk.
Да, сделайте пересадку в Смоленске.
dah, ZDEH-leye-t'eh p'i-r'i-SAHT-koo FSMAW-l'in-sk'eh.

What is your name?
Как вас зовут?
kahk vahs zuh-VOOT?

My name is ———.
Меня зовут ———.
m'i-N'AH zuh-VOOT ———.

Your first name (family name)?
Ваше имя (ваша фамилия)?
VAH-sheh EE-m'uh (VAH-shuh fuh-M'EE-l'i-yuh)?

Are you alone?
Вы один (одна)?
vy uh-D'EEN (uhd-NAH)?

Yes, I am alone.
Да, я один (одна).
dah, yah uh-D'EEN (uhd-NAH).

No, I am traveling with my husband (wife).
Нет, я путешествую с мужем (с женой).
n'eht, yah poo-t'i-SHEHST-voo-yoo SMOO-zhym (szhy-NOI).

How many of you are there?
Сколько вас?
SKAWL'-kuh vahs?

There are five of us.
Нас пятеро.
nahs P'AH-t'i-ruh.

Have you a passport?
У вас есть паспорт?
oo vahs yehst' PAHS-puhrt?

Here is my passport.
Вот мой паспорт.
vawt moi PAHS-puhrt.

Where were you born?
Где вы родились?
gd'eh vy ruh-D'EE-l'is?

I was born in America.
Я родился (родилась) в Америке.
yah ruh-D'EEL-s'uh (ruh-D'EE-LAHS') vh-

What is your nationality?
Какой вы национальности?
kuh-KOI vy nuh-tsyuh-NAHL'-nuhs-t'ee?

I am an American.
Я американец (американка).
yah uh-m'i-r'i-KAH-n'ehts (uh-m'i-r'i-KAHN-kuh).

Where is your health certificate?
Где ваше медицинское свидетельство?
gd'eh VAH-sheh m'i-d'i-TSYN-skuh-yeh sv'i-D'EH-t'il's-tvuh?

Here it is.
Вот оно.
VAWT-uh-NAW.

May I see your permit?
Могу я посмотреть ваш пропуск?
muh-GOO yah puh-smuh-TR'EHT' vahsh PRAW-poosk?

Here is my permit.
Вот мой пропуск.
VAWT-moi PRAW-poosk.

Here are my documents.
Вот мои документы.
vawt muh-YEE duh-koo-M'EHN-ty.

Here they are.
Вот они.
VAWT uh-N'EE.

CUSTOMS

Must I pay duty on this?
Обязан (обязана) я заплатить пошлину за это?
uh-B'AH-zuhn (uh-B'AH-zuh-nuh) yah zuh-pluh-T'EET'
  PAWSH-l'i-noo zuh EH-tuh?

Must I open this bag?
Должен (должна) ли я открыть этот чемодан?
DAWL-zhyn (duhl-ZHNAH) l'i yah uht-KRYT' EH-tuht chi-
  muh-DAHN?

How much must I pay?
Сколько я должен (должна) заплатить?
SKAWL'-kuh yah DAWL-zhyn (duhl-ZHNAH) zuh-pluh-
  T'EET'?

You must pay twenty rubles.
Вы должны заплатить двадцать рублей.
vy duhl-ZHNY zuh-pluh-T'EET' DVAH-tsuht' roo-BL'EY.

Have you anything (else) to declare?
Имеете ли вы что нибудь (ещё) предъявить для пошлины?
ee-M'EH-yi-t'eh l'i vy SHTAW-n'i-boot' (yish-CHAW) pr'id-
  yuh-V'EET' dl'uh PAWSH-l'i-ny?

I have nothing (else) to declare.
У меня ничего нет (больше) предъявить.
oo m'i-N'AH n'i-chi-VAW n'eht (BAWL'-sheh) pr'id-yuh-
  V'EET'.

Is that all?
Это всё?
EH-tuh-FS'AW?

That's all.
Это всё.
EH-tuh-FS'AW.

I cannot open this valise (trunk).
Я не могу открыть этот саквояж (сундук).
yah n'i muh-GOO uht-KRYT' EH-tuht suhk-vuh-YAHZH
  (soon-DOOK).

I have lost the key.
Я потерял (потеряла) ключ.
yah puh-t'i-R'AHL (puh-t'i-R'AH-luh) kl'ooch.

Where can I have a new key made?
Где я могу заказать новый ключ?
gd'eh yah muh-GOO zuh-kuh-ZAHT' NAW-vy kl'ooch?

The locksmith is in the next street.
Слесарь на улице рядом.
SL'EH-suhr' nuh OO-l'i-ts'eh R'AH-duhm.

Please be careful.
Пожалуйста будьте осторожны.
puh-ZHAHL-stuh BOOT'-t'eh uhs-tuh-RAWZH-ny.

Please help me close this bag.
Помогите мне пожалуйста закрыть этот чемодан.
puh-muh-G'EE-t'eh mn'eh puh-ZHAHL-stuh zuh-KRYT' EH-tuht chi-muh-DAHN.

This is (not) dutiable.
Это (не) подлежит оплате пошлиной.
EH-tuh (n'i) puhd-l'i-ZHYT uh-PLAH-t'eh PAWSH-l'i-noi.

I am on a pleasure trip.
Я путешествую для удовольствия.
yah poo-t'i-SHEHST-voo-yoo dl'uh oo-duh-VAWL'-stv'i-yuh.

This article is for personal use.
Этот предмет для личного употребления.
EH-tuht pr'id-M'EHT dl'uh L'EECH-nuh-vuh oo-puh-tr'i-BL'EH-n'i-yuh.

Where is your baggage?
Где ваш багаж?
gd'eh vahsh buh-GAHSH?

Here is my baggage.
Вот мой багаж.
vawt moi buh-GAHSH.

Those are my bags.
Это мои чемоданы.
EH-tuh muh-YEE chi-muh-DAH-ny.

I cannot find my baggage.
Я не могу найти мой багаж.
yah n'i muh-GOO neye-T'EE moi buh-GAHSH.

152

Where is the customs office?
Где таможня?
gd'eh tuh-MAWZH-n'uh?

Here is the customs office.
Таможня тут.
tuh-MAWZH-n'uh toot.

These articles are gifts.
Эти вещи—подарки.
EH-t'ee V'EHSH-chee puh-DAHR-kee.

Must I fill out this form?
Я должен (должна) заполнить этот формуляр?
yah DAWL-zhyn (duhl-ZHNAH) zuh-PAWL-n'it' EH-tuht
fuhr-moo-L'AHR?

Please fill out this form.
Заполните пожалуйста этот формуляр.
zuh-PAWL-n'i-t'eh puh-ZHAHL-stuh EH-tuht fuhr-moo-
L'AHR.

Have you any foreign currency?
Есть ли у вас иностранные деньги?
yehst' l'i oo vahs ee-nuh-STRAHN-ny-yeh D'EHN'-g'ee?

How much foreign currency have you?
Сколько у вас иностранных денег?
SKAWL'-kuh oo vahs ee-nuh-STRAHN-nykh D'EH-n'ik?

I have $500 in U.S. currency.
У меня пятсот долларов в американской валюте.
oo m'i-N'AH p'uht-SAWT duh-luh-RAWF vuh-m'i-r'i-KAHN-
skoi vuh-L'OO-t'eh.

May I close the bag (trunk) now?
Могу ли я теперь закрыть чемодан (сундук)?
muh-GOO l'i yah t'i-P'EHR' zuh-KRYT' chi-muh-DAHN
(soon-DOOK)?

You may close it (them).
Вы можете его (их) закрыть.
vy MAW-zhy-t'eh yi-VAW (eekh) zuh-KRYT'.

24
BAGGAGE

I want a porter.
Мне нужен носильщик.
mn'eh NOO-zhyn nuh-S'EEL'-shchik.

I want to insure (check) my baggage.
Я хочу застраховать (сдать на хранение) мой багаж.
yah khuh-CHOO zuh-struh-khuh-VAHT' (zdaht' nuh khruh-N'EH-n'yeh) moi buh-GAHSH.

I want to check this trunk to Leningrad.
Я хочу сдать этот сундук в багаж в Ленинград.
yah khuh-CHOO zdaht' EH-tuht soon-DOOK vbuh-GAHSH vl'i-n'in-GRAHT.

I want to leave my bags here (take out my bag).
Я хочу оставить чемоданы здесь (взять мой чемодан).
yah khuh-CHOO uhs-TAH-v'it' chi-muh-DAH-ny zd'ch (vz'aht' moi chi-muh-DAHN).

Where is the baggage room?
Где комната для хранения багажа?
gd'eh KAWM-nuh-tuh dl'uh khruh-N'EH-n'i-yuh buh-guh-ZHAH?

This is my bag (trunk).
Вот мой чемодан (сундук).
vawt moi chi-muh-DAHN (soon-DOOK).

These are our bags (trunks).
Это наши чемоданы (сундуки).
EH-tuh NAH-shy chi-muh-DAH-ny (soon-doo-K'EE).

This is not my baggage.
Это не мой багаж.
EH-tuh n'eh-moi buh-GAHSH.

What is the rate per bag?
Какой тариф за каждую вещь багажа?
kuh-KOI tuh-R'EEF zuh KAHZH-doo-yoo v'ehshch buh-guh-ZHAH?

How many pieces of baggage?
Сколько мест багажа?
SKAWL'-kuh m'ehst buh-guh-ZHAH?

Give me a receipt.
Дайте мне расписку.
DEYE-t'eh mn'eh ruhs-P'EES-koo.

Here is a tip.
Вот на чай.
vawt nuh-CHEYE.

Please call me a taxi.
Позовите пожалуйста такси.
puh-zuh-V'EE-t'eh puh-ZHAHL-suh tuhk-S'EE.

Bring it (them) over here.
Принесите это (их) сюда.
pr'i-n'i-S'EE-t'eh EH-tuh (eekh) s'oo-DAH.

Put it (them) over there.
Положите это (их) туда.
puh-luh-ZHY-t'eh EH-tuh (eekh) too-DAH.

Here are my baggage checks.
Вот мои багажные квитанции.
vawt muh-YEE buh-GAHZH-ny-yeh kv'i-TAHN-tsee-i.

Take me (us) to the hotel.
Везите меня (нас) в отель.
v'i-Z'EE-t'eh m'i-N'AH (nahs) vuh-T'EHL'.

Must I wait?
Я должен (должна) подождать?
yah DAWL-zhyn (duhl-ZHNAH) puh-duhzh-DAHT'?

Must I pay excess weight?
Должен (должна) ли я заплатить за лишний вес?
DAWL-zhyn (duhl-ZHNAH) l'i yah zuh-pluh-T'EET' zu L'EESH-n'ee v'ehs?

Shall I pay now or later?
Должен (должна) ли я заплатить сейчас или после?
DAWL-zhyn (duhl-ZHNAH) l'i yah zuh-pluh-T'EET' s'e CHAHS EE-l'ee PAWS-l'eh?

Please don't break the seals.
Пожалуйста не поломайте печати.
puh-ZHAHL-stuh n'eh puh-luh-MEYE-t'eh p'i-CHAH-t'ee.

Please carry that bag carefully.
Пожалуйста несите этот чемодан осторожно.
puh-ZHAHL-stuh n'i-S'EE-t'eh EH-tuht chi-muh-DAHN uhs
   tuh-RAWZH-nuh.

Take it (them) to a taxi.
Отнесите это (эти вещи) в такси.
uht-n'i-S'EE-t'eh EH-tuh (EH-t'ee V'EHSH-chee) ftuhk-S'EE

TRANSLATION

Где сидят Том и Мэри?
Где работает врач?
Где работает учитель?
Где работает агроном?
Где работает инженер?
Где живёт ваша семья?
Где живёт Джон?
Где живут студенты?
Где стоит лампа?
Где лежат тетради?

Где стоит шкаф?
Где лежат ваши вещи?
Где лежит ковёр?
Где вы любите гулять?
Где она обычно отдыхает?
Где сейчас его сестра?
Где стоит поезд?
О чём рассказывает Миша?
О чём ты спрашиваешь?
О чём она спрашивает?

Я покупаю в киоске *газету*.
Мы видим *деревню*.
Я люблю *маму*.
Я слушаю *брата*.
Они слушают *учителя*.
Я открываю *тетрадь*.
Он любит *мать*.

Я вижу этот *дом*.
Мы читали этот *журнал*.
Я вижу его *словарь*.
Мы знаем этот *санаторий*.
Я хорошо знаю это *правило*.

159

Т: Скажи́те, пожа́луйста, ско́лько сто́ит э́тот сыр?
П: Три рубля́ килогра́мм.
Т: А ско́лько сто́ит э́та колбаса́?
П: Два рубля́ 50 копе́ек килогра́мм.
Т: Спаси́бо! Джон, что ты хо́чешь: сыр или колбасу́?
Д: Колбасу́.
Т: Хорошо́. Скажи́те, пожа́луйста, где ка́сса?
П: Ка́сса напра́во.
Т: Спаси́бо!

Вот ко́мната. Это класс. Сле́ва окно́, спра́ва дверь.
Здесь шкаф. Там доска́.
Вот стол. Здесь кни́га, тетра́дь, ру́чка и каранда́ш.
А э́то стул.
Это Том. Он студе́нт. Это Эми́лия. Она́ студе́нтка.
Эми́лия спра́шивает, а Том отвеча́ет.
— Что э́то?
— Это ла́мпа.
— Это портфе́ль?
— Да, э́то портфе́ль.
— Это слова́рь?
— Да.
— Это уче́бник?
— Нет, э́то не уче́бник, а тетра́дь.
— Кто э́то?
— Это студе́нтка.
Тепе́рь спра́шивает Том, а Эми́лия отвеча́ет.
— Где дверь?
— Она́ спра́ва.
— Где окно́?
— Оно́ сле́ва.

Откуда вы приехали?

Откуда приехал ваш друг?

Откуда вы пришли?

Откуда вы идёте?

От кого вы получили письмо?

———

Африка, Америка, Уганда, Кения, Нигерия, Индия
север, юг, восток, запад, Кавказ, Занзибар
завод, фабрика, работа, выставка, концерт, вечер, экскурсия, прогулка, вокзал, станция, почта, телеграф, стадион
класс, аудитория, лаборатория, комната, институт, университет, поликлиника, клуб, театр, магазин, музей
мать, отец, брат, сестра, друг, подруга, дядя, тётя, товарищи, родители

———

Днём уро́ки. Мы чита́ем и пи́шем по-ру́сски.
Пото́м мы обе́даем.
— А когда́ вы обе́даете?
— Днём.

Сейча́с у́тро. У́тром Том за́втракает.
— А что де́лает Эми́лия?
— То́же за́втракает.

161

Ми́ша, это твоя́ ко́мната?

Да.

Кто ещё здесь живёт?

Студе́нт из Уга́нды Джо́зеф. Его́ крова́ть напра́во в углу́.

А где его́ ве́щи?

В шкафу́.

А чьи кни́ги на по́лке?

Мои́ и его́.

А э́то чья карти́на?

Моя́. Это дере́вня, где я живу́.

Там о́чень краси́во.

Да. Ви́дишь ря́дом лес и река́. Я о́чень люблю́ гуля́ть в лесу́. Я всегда́ отдыха́ю то́лько там.

———

Я занима́юсь спо́ртом (физкуль-
*   ту́рой).*

Чем вы занима́етесь?

Он занима́ется медици́ной.

Она́ угости́ла меня́ ча́ем.

Он боле́ет гри́ппом.

Моя́ сестра́ интересу́ется му́зы-
*   кой.*

Мы бы́ли дово́льны жи́знью в
*   гора́х.*

Я не согла́сен с ним.

Что с ней случи́лось?

Что с ва́ми (случи́лось)?

Роди́тели рассерди́лись на сы́на.

(Поздравля́ю вас) с пра́здником!

Поздравля́ю вас с днём рожде́ния!

Поздравля́ю вас с Но́вым го́дом!

Поздравля́ю вас с Междунаро́дным
*   Же́нским днём.*

Поздравля́ю вас с пра́здником
*   Пе́рвого Ма́я.*

———

*Мой друг сказа́л мне: «Ве́чером
    я бу́ду до́ма».*
*Мой друг сказа́л мне, что ве́-
    чером он бу́дет до́ма.*
*Он спроси́л меня́: «Где вы жи-
    вёте?»*
Он спроси́л меня́, где я живу́.

*Я спроси́л профе́ссора: «Сего́дня
    бу́дет ле́кция?»*
*Я спроси́л профе́ссора, бу́дет ли
    сего́дня ле́кция.*

*Това́рищ спроси́л меня́: «Ты хо-
    рошо́ отдохну́л ле́том?»*
*Това́рищ спроси́л меня́, хорошо́
    ли я отдохну́л ле́том.*

———

Студенты встретились *с профессо-
ром.*
Девушка разговаривала *с преподава-
телем.*
Больной посоветовался *с товари-
щем.*
Мы познакомились *с алжирцем.*
Он поздоровался *с мужчиной.*
Дети попрощались *с тётей.*
Ученики поздоровались *с учитель-
ницей.*

———

"Do you speak Russian?"
"Yes, a little."
"Is it your watch?"
"No, it is not mine."
"What is the time?"
"It is one o'clock (two o'clock)."
The students like to look at television in the evening.

The movement for Indo-Soviet friendship was born spontaneously. Its appearance was conditioned historically, and organisationally it was formalised at a time the Soviet people were waging a heroic struggle against the nazi onslaught. Today this movement is one of the largest in my country.

The cooperation between the Union of Friendship Societies and the friendship societies of the socialist community countries, including the Hungarian-Soviet Friendship Society, is becoming more and more fruitful. Our society is proud of its mission of acquainting the Hungarian public with the rich history and culture of the Soviet Union and with its scientific and technological achievements.

In virtually every country societies of friendship with the Soviet Union constitute a force of truth and, consequently, a force of peace, which is why it is imperative to consolidate these forces.

The point is, within a few minutes of the "first strike," which your military experts are now discussing with such boldness, in other words, within a few minutes of the time my home is destroyed, your home won't exist either.

No one will be able to shelter from the common disaster that threatens our planet, will be able to sit it out, not across the widest oceans, not behind the highest mountains. The disaster will strike even the ultra-non-aligned, the ultra-neutral countries. Not at once, perhaps, but it is bound to strike.

It is bitter and painful to think that our great earthly civilization, together with the age-old culture of our planet, will be turned into dust, into nothingness, into radioactive ashes!

This must not be allowed to happen, my coeval! Must not!

We must stop, my coeval.

We must curb this hellish, mad pace of the arms race, we must curb it at all costs!

Panchmarhi means five caves. Legends say that the Pandavas of the Mahabharata fame lived 12 years of their exile there. But others have a belief that these are the Buddhist viharas. Panchmarhi is a beautiful hill girdled plateau on the Satpura hills. It is never too cold in winter and never too hot in summer with its dozen waterfull and 60 view points. The five caves and the bathing pools are the main attractions. There is a decent golf course at Panchmarhi club.

Ujjain is a great pilgrimage and one of the most holy cities of the Hindus. People from all over India come to Ujjain, which stands on the banks of the river Shipra, to see the Kumbh Mela which is held every twelve years. Though during Ashoka's reign, Ujjain was a great centre of Buddhism but it is famous as the legendary King Vikramaditya's capital, in whose court flourished the 'nine jewels' of Hindu literature among whom Kalidas, was the foremost.

Sanchi is famous for its bell shaped monuments, stupas, which were funeral mounds or Tamili. The bodies of Buddha and other sages were cremated on pyre and the bones collected and taken to different pilgrimages where they were intered in stupas. Buddha was represented by symbols in the early Buddhist period. Symbols were of lotus, representing his miraculous birth, the peepal tree, signifying his attaining enlightment under this tree at Bodh Gaya, the wheel, derived from the title of the first sermon entitled "the turning of the wheel of law", and lastly the stupa to represent his death. His footprints and throne were also sometimes used to denote Buddha's presence.

RUSSIAN
VOCABULARY

Аа

a and, but
абрикос apricot
август August
австриец Austrian
австрийский (adj.) Austrian
автобус bus
автомобиль car, automobile
ад hell
адрес address
акселератор accelerator
Америка America
американец American
американский (adj.) American
ананас pineapple
английская булавка safety pin
английский English
англичанин Englishman
Англия England
апельсин orange
аперитив apéritif
апрель April
аптека drugstore
араб Arab
арабский Arabic, Arabian
арбуз watermelon
аргентинец Argentinian
аргентинский (adj.) Argentinian
аспирин aspirin
аэродром airport, airfield
аэролиния airline
аэроплан airplane

Бб

багаж baggage, luggage
багажная комната baggage room
багажное отделение trunk compartment (car)
багажный вагон baggage car
базар market
бал ball (dance)
балкон theater balcony
банан banana
банк bank
банка can, tin

батарея car battery
беде (быть в . . .) to be in trouble
бедный poor
бедро hip, thigh
бегать to run
без without
баранина lamb, mutton
бархат velvet
барышня Miss, young lady
бассейн для плаванья swimming pool
безопасная бритва safety razor
беж tan
бежать to run (with specific goal)
белило clothes bleach
белый white
бельгиец Belgian
бельгийский (adj.) Belgian
бельё underwear
бензин gas(oline)
бензиновая помпа fuel pump
бензиновая станция gas (service) station
берегитесь! look out!, watch out!, careful!
беспокойство bother, worry
беспокойтесь (не . . . !) don't worry, don't bother, don't trouble yourself!
библиотека library
билет ticket
билет туда и обратно round-trip ticket
билетная касса box (ticket) office
биллион billion
бинокль field (opera) glasses
бифштекс steak
благодарить to thank
благодарный grateful
бланк blank, form (document)
близ (prep.) close, near
близкий (adj.) close, near
близко (adv.) near, close
блузка blouse
блюдечко saucer
блюдо dish, course (in meal)
бобы beans
богатый rich
более more
болезнь illness
болеть to hurt
болт bolt (car)
боль в животе stomach-ache

боль в ухе earache
больница hospital
больной ill, sick
больше more, bigger
большой big, large
большой палец thumb
большой палец ноги big toe
борная кислота boric acid
борту (на . . .) on board
ботинок shoe
бояться to fear, to be afraid
бразильянец Brazilian
бразильянский (adj.) Brazilian
браслет bracelet
брат brother
брать to take
брать за to charge
бритва razor
бритвенный нож razor blade
бриться to shave oneself
бровь eyebrow
брюки pants, trousers
будильник alarm clock
будить to waken, rouse
будка phone booth
будущий coming, next, future
будьте осторожны! look out!, be careful!
булавка pin
булка, булочка roll (bread)
бумага paper
бумажник man's pocketbook
бураки beets
бутерброд sandwich
бутылка bottle
был, была, было was
были were
быстро quickly
быстрый quick
быть to be, exist
бюстгальтер bra, brassière

Вв

в in, on, at
вагон railroad coach, car
вагон для курящих smoking car
вагон-ресторан dining car

валюта currency
вам to you
ванна bath
ванная bathroom
ванный коврик bath mat
варёный boiled, cooked
варенье jam
варить to cook, boil
вас you
вата absorbent cotton
ваш your
вверх up, upward (motion)
вдруг suddenly
веер fan
вежливый polite
веко eyelid
великий great
величина size
венгерец Hungarian
венгерский Hungarian (adj.)
вентилятор car fan
верёвка rope, string
верить to believe
вернуться to be back (perf.)
верный sure, true
верх top
верхний upper
вес weight
весёлый merry, gay
весить to weigh
весна spring (season)
ветер wind
ветеринар veterinary
ветренный windy
ветрено it is windy
ветчина ham
вечер evening
   добрый . . . good evening
   до вечера see you this evening
   вечером in the evening
вечерний ресторан night club
вечерняя одежда evening clothes
вешалка coat hanger
вещь article, thing
взять to take (perf.)
взять на буксир to tow (perf.)
вид view, sight
видеть to see
вилка fork
вино wine
виноват excuse me, I beg your pardon, I'm sorry
виноград grapes

170

винтовой ключ wrench
виски whiskey
витрина display window
вишня cherry
включатель electric switch
включённый included, plugged in
вкусный tasty
влажный damp, humid
вместе together
вместо instead of
внезапно suddenly
внезапный sudden
вниз down, downstairs (motion)
внизу down, downstairs (location)
внутри inside (location)
внутрь inside (motion)
во (see в)
вода water
    ... со льдом ice water
водевиль vaudeville
водка vodka
возвратить деньги to refund (perf.)
возвратиться to be back, get back, come back, return (perf.)
возвращать деньги to refund
возвращаться to be back, get back, come back, return
воздух air
воздушная почта air mail
возможный possible
войдите! come in!
войлок felt (material)
войти to come in, go in, walk in, enter (perf.)
вокзал railroad station, terminal
волос hair
вон out
вон! "scram"!
вор thief
ворота gate
воротник collar
восемнадцать eighteen
восемь eight
восемьдесят eighty
воскресенье Sunday
воспрещается (it) is forbidden
восток East
восьмой eighth
вот here is, are; there is, there are
вперёд forward, ahead (motion)
впереди ahead, in front (location)
впору (быть ...) to fit
врач docto

временно temporarily, for the time being
время time
    во ... on time
время года season
все all, everybody, everyone
всё all, everything
всегда always
вставать to get up, rise
встать to get up, rise (perf.)
встретить to meet (perf.)
встречать to meet
всюду everywhere
всякий each, every
вторник Tuesday
второй second
вход entrance
вход воспрещается no admittance
входить to go in, come in, walk in, enter
вчера yesterday
вы you
выбирать to choose, select
выбрать to choose, select (perf.)
вывеска sign
вывих sprain
выздоравливать to recover (health)
выздороветь to recover (health) (perf.)
выйти (perf.) to go out, come out, walk out, leave
вымыться to wash oneself (perf.)
выпивка drink (noun)
высадиться to land from ship (perf.)
высаживаться to land from ship
высокий tall, high
выставка showcase, exhibition
выхлопная труба exhaust (car)
выход exit
выходить to come out, go out, walk out, leave

Гг

гавань harbor
газ gauze
газета newspaper
газетный киоск newstand
гайка nut (mechanical)

171

галёрка theater gallery
галлерея art gallery
галоши rubbers, galoshes
галстук necktie
гараж garage
гарнир vegetables
где where (location)
гектограмм hectogram
гид guide
гладить to press, iron
глаз eye
глубокий deep
говорить to speak, talk, say, tell
говядина beef
год year
годный для питья drinkable
голландец Hollander
голландский Dutch
голова head
головная боль headache
головная щётка hairbrush
голодный hungry
голос voice
голубой light blue
гора mountain, hill
гореть to burn
горло throat
горничная maid
город city, town
горох peas
горький bitter
горячий hot (burning)
госпиталь hospital
господин Mr., sir, gentleman
госпожа Mrs., lady
гостиная living room, parlor
гостиница hotel
готовый ready
град (идёт . . .) it is hailing
гражданин Mr.
гражданка Miss (in address)
грамм gram
гребёнка comb
грейпфрут grapefruit
грек Greek
греческий Greek (adj.)
гриб mushroom
гром thunder
груша pear
грязный dirty
губа lip
губка sponge
губная помада lipstick
гулять to take a walk, go strolling

густой thick (dense)
гусь goose

Дд

да yes
давать to give, let
далёкий far, distant (adj.)
далеко far, far away (adv.)
дальше что? what next?
дама lady
дамская парикмахерская beauty salon, parlor
дамская уборная ladies' room, powder room
датский Danish
датчанин Dane
дать to give, let (perf.)
два two
двадцать twenty
дважды twice
двенадцать twelve
дверь door
двигать to move
двинуть to move (perf.)
двойные кровати twin beds
двор courtyard
дворец palace
девичий монастырь convent

девочка little girl
девушка girl, young lady
девяносто ninety
девятнадцать nineteen
девятый ninth
девять nine
дед (or дедушка) grandfather
дезодоратор deodorant
действительно really, actually
действительный good for (valid)
декабрь December
декларация declaration
делать to do, make
дело thing, affair, matter
день day
деньги money
деревня country
  в деревне in the country
дерево tree, wood

держать to keep, hold
держаться to last
держите трубку hold the wire
десерт dessert
десна gums
десятый tenth
десять ten
дешёвая распродажа bargain sale
дешёвый cheap, inexpensive
джин gin
диван sofa
директор manager
дисентерия dysentery
длинна length
длинный long (object)
для for
днём in the afternoon
дня p.m.
до to, until, till
до востребования general delivery
до свидания good-by, till we meet
    again
добрый good, kind
довольно enough, rather
догореть to burn (perf.)
дождевик raincoat
дождь rain
дождь идёт it is raining
док dock
доктор doctor
документ document
долгий long (time)
должен must
должным (быть . . .) to owe
доллар dollar
дом house, home
дом для молодёжи youth hostel
дома at home
домашний domestic
домкрат car jack
домой homeward, home (motion)
дорога road
дорогой dear, expensive
дорогу! gangway!
дороже more expensive
дорожка plane runway
дорожная карта road map
доставить to deliver, provide (perf.)
доставка delivery
доставлять to deliver, provide
достаточно enough
дочь daughter
драгоценности jewelry

друг friend
другой other, another, different
думать to think
дура dumbbell (fem.) (slang)
дурак dumbbell (slang)
духи perfume
душ shower (bath)
дым smoke
дыня melon
дышать to breathe
дюжина dozen
дядя uncle

Ее   Её

еврей Hebrew, Jew
еврейский Hebrew, Jewish
его his, him
еда meal, food
её her
езда ride
ездить to drive, go (conveyance)
ему him, to him
ерунда! nonsense!
если if
есть there is, are, is
есть to eat
ехать to travel, ride
ещё still, yet
    не . . . not yet

Жж

жалоба complaint
жаловаться to complain
жаль pity
    как . . .! what a pity!, too bad!
жара heat
жареный fried, broiled, roasted
жаркий hot (weather)
жарко it is hot (weather)
жаркое roast
жаркое из говядины roast beef

ждать to wait, expect
желать to want, wish, desire
железная дорога railroad
железо iron (metal)
жёлтый yellow
жена wife
женщина woman
жёсткий tough (meat)
жетон token (bus, streetcar, phone)
живой living, alive
живот stomach
животное animal
жидкость liquid
жидкость для зажигалки lighter
    fluid
жидкость для удаления лака
    polish remover
жизнь life
жилет vest
жить to live
журнал magazine

Зз

за behind, after, beyond, ago, in
    exchange for
забота care
забывать to forget
забыть to forget (perf.)
завернуть to wrap up (perf.)
завёртывать to wrap up
завивка finger wave
завтра tomorrow
завтрак lunch
завтрак в корзинке lunch basket
завтракать to have lunch
задняя сигнальная лампочка tail
    light (car)
загородный разговор long-distance
    call
зайти за to come for (perf.)
зажечь to light (perf.)
зажигалка cigarette lighter
зажигание ignition (car)
зажигать to light
заказ order, reservation
заказать to order, reserve (perf.)

заказное письмо registered letter
заказные письма registry window,
    registered mail
заказывать to order, reserve
закон law
закрывать to close, shut
закрытый closed
закрыть to close, shut (perf.)
закусить to get a bite (perf.)
закуска appetizer
закусывать to get a bite
замок castle
замок lock
занимать to borrow
занят busy, taken, occupied
занятой occupied
занять to borrow (perf.)
запад west
запасная шина spare tire
запечатать to seal (perf.)
запечатывать to seal
запломбировать to fill a tooth (perf.)
запломбировывать to fill a tooth
заполнить to fill out (perf.)
заполнять to fill out
запомнить to remember (perf.)
запонки cuff links
запрещается (it) is forbidden
запрещённый forbidden
запястье wrist, bracelet
засмеяться to laugh (perf.)
заставать to find, reach a person
заставить to have something done
    (perf.)
заставлять to have something done
застать to find, reach a person (perf.)
застраховать to insure (perf.)
заходить за to come for
захотеть to wish, want (perf.)
звать to call, page
звезда star
звонить to ring
звонок bell
здание building
здесь here
здоровье (на . . .) to your health!
здравствуйте! hello!
зелёный green
земля earth, land
земляника strawberry
зеркало mirror
зима winter
зипер zipper

знать to know (person or fact)
значить to mean (thing as subject)
золото gold
зонтик umbrella, parasol
зоологический сад zoo
зуб tooth
зубная боль toothache
зубная паста toothpaste
зубная щётка toothbrush
зубной dental
зубной врач dentist

Ии

и and, also
иголка needle
игра game
играть в to play (games)
играть на to play (music)
идти to go (on foot), walk
идти за покупками to go shopping
из out, from (within)
избегать to avoid
избежать to avoid (perf.)
извините excuse me, pardon me,
    I'm sorry
извозчик coachman
икра caviar
или or
иметь to have, own, possess
иметь связь to be connected (phone)
имущество belongings
имя first name
индюшка turkey
иногда sometimes
иной different
иностранный foreign
интересный interesting
иод iodine
искать to look for
искренний sincere
искусство art
испанец Spaniard
испанский Spanish
истолкователь interpreter
итальянец Italian
итальянский Italian (adj.)
июль July
июнь June

Кк

казаться to seem, appear
как how, as, like
как далеко how far
как долго how long
какой which
какой-нибудь any
калоши rubbers
кальсоны shorts
камера inner tube
канадец Canadian
канадский Canadian (adj.)
капитан captain
капот hood (car)
капуста cabbage
карандаш pencil
карбюратор carburetor
карман pocket
карманный pocket (adj.)
карта playing card
картина picture (art)
картофель potato(es)
карточка visiting card
касса box office, window (bank,
    post office, theater)
кассир cashier, teller (bank)
касторовое масло castor oil
католик Catholic
католический Catholic (adj.)
катушка фильмов roll of film
каша porridge, gruel, groats
кашель cough
кашлять to cough
каштан chestnut
каюта stateroom
квадратный square
квартал city block
квартира apartment
квитанция receipt, baggage check
кекс cake
килограмм kilogram
кисет tobacco pouch
кислый sour
кисточка для бритья shaving brush
кисть wrist
китаец Chinese
китайский Chinese (adj.)
класс class
класть to put, place
ключ key

кляксон car horn
книга book
книжный магазин bookstore
ко (see к)
ковёр rug
когда when
кого whom, whose
кожа skin, leather
койка berth
коктель cocktail
колбаса sausage
колд крэм cold cream
колено knee
колесо wheel
кольцо ring (ornament)
комар mosquito, gnat
комедия comedy
комната room
комната для двоих double room
комната для одного single room
комната для хранения багажа (or
    багажная комната) check room
компания company
кому to whom?
конверт envelope
кондуктор conductor (car or train)
конец end
конечная станция terminal (bus or
    plane)
конечно of course, certainly, sure,
    you bet!
консерв can
консул consul
консульство consulate
контора office
контора потерянных вещей lost-
    and-found
конфета candy
концерт concert
кончать to finish, end
кончить to finish, end (perf.)
конь horse
копейка kopek (1/100 of a ruble)
корабль ship, boat
корень root
корзинка basket
коридорный bellboy, bellhop
коричневый brown
коробка box, package
коробка скоростей clutch (car)
королевский royal
короткий short
корсет girdle

кость bone
костюм suit
кот tomcat
котлета cutlet
который which
кофе coffee
кошелёк wallet, purse
кошка cat
красивый pretty, beautiful
краска для волос hair tint
красный red
красть to rob, steal
крахмал starch
крахмалить to starch
креветка shrimp
кредитный билет bill (banknote)
кремень flint (lighter)
кресло armchair, easy chair
кресло в партере orchestra seat
кривая curve
кровать bed
кровь blood
круглый round
кружево lace
крутой steep
крыло автомобиля fender
крэм для бритья shaving cream
крючок hook
кто who
кто-нибудь anyone, anybody
кто-то someone, somebody
кубанец Cuban
кубанский Cuban (adj.)
кувшин pitcher
куда where (motion)
кукуруза Indian corn, maize
купальная шапочка bathing cap
купальный костюм bathing suit
купальный халат bathrobe
купаться to bathe, swim
купить to buy, purchase
купэ compartment
курить to smoke
курить воспрещается smoking for-
    bidden
курица chicken, hen
курс rate of exchange
кусок piece
кухня kitchen
кучер coachman
кушанье food, dish, meal
кушать to eat

любить to love
любой any
люди people, men

Лл

лавка shop
лак для ногтей nail polish
лампа lamp
лампочка electric bulb
латук lettuce
левый left (opposite of right)
лёгкий easy, light, mild
лёгкое lung
легче! take it easy!
лёд ice
лезть climb
лекарство medicine
лекарство от кашля cough syrup
лента ribbon
лес woods
лестница stairs
летать to fly
лето summer
лечь to lie down (perf.)
либо or
ликёр liqueur
лиловый purple
лимон lemon
лимонад lemonade
линия line
лист sheet of paper, leaf
литр liter
лифт elevator
лихорадка fever
лицо face
личный personal
лишний вес excess weight
лоб forehead
ловить to catch
ложиться to lie down
ложка spoon(ful)
локоть elbow
ломать to break
лошадь horse
лук onion
луна moon, month
лучше better
лучший best
любезный kind

Мм

магазин store
магазин духов perfume shop
магазин обуви shoe store
магазин шляп hat shop
май May
маленький little, small
мальчик boy
мандарин tangerine
маникюр manicure
маникюристка manicurist
марка stamp, postage
март March
маслина black olive
масло butter, oil
массаж massage
массаж головы scalp massage
материя cloth
матрац mattress
мать mother
машина car, automobile
машинка barber's clippers
мебель furniture
меблированный furnished
медицинский medical
медленнее more slowly
медленно slowly
медленный slow
между between, among
мексиканец Mexican
мексиканский Mexican (adj.)
мелочи small change
мелочь change
мена exchange
меньше less
меню menu
менялная контора exchange office
менять to cash, change, exchange
мёртвый dead
местный domestic
местный разговор local phone call
место place, seat

177

месяц month, moon

метр meter

метр д'отель headwaiter

механик mechanic

милиционер policeman

миллион million

милый sweet, dear

миндаль almonds (collective plural)

минеральная вода mineral water

минута minute

много much, many, lots of, a great deal

может-быть maybe, perhaps

можно вам помочь? may I help you?

мой my

мокрый wet

молния lightning

молодой young

молоко milk

молоток hammer

монастырь monastery

монета coin

монумент monument

море sea

морковь carrot

мороженое ice cream

морозит it is freezing

моросит it is drizzling

морская болезнь seasickness

москит mosquito

мост bridge

мотор engine, motor

мочь to be able, can

муж husband

мужская уборная men's room

мужчина man

музей museum

мундштук cigarette holder

мы we

мыло soap

мыло в порошке soap flakes

мыться to wash oneself

мягкая бумага tissue paper

мягкий soft

мясо meat

мяч ball (playing)

Нн

на on, in, for

наверх up, upstairs (motion)

наверху up, upstairs (location)

наволочка pillow case

над over, above

надевать to put on

надеть to put on (perf.)

надеяться to hope

надо need

надоеда, надоедливый pest (slang)

назад back, backward, ago

найти to find (perf.)

найтись to be, be found (perf.)

налево to the left

налейте! fill her up! (car)

наличные деньги cash

налог tax

нам to us

нанимать to hire

нанять to hire (perf.)

напильник для ногтей nail file

напиток drink

наполнить to fill (perf.)

наполнять to fill

направить to direct (perf.)

направление direction

направлять to direct

направо to the right

нарезать to cut (perf.)

наруже outside (location)

наружу outside, outward

нарыв abscess

нас us

насекомое insect

нахальство (какое...) what nerve!

находить to find

находиться to be, be found

национальность nationality

начай tip, gratuity

начальник станции stationmaster

начать to begin, start (perf.)

начинать to begin, start

наш our, ours

не not

неалкогольный напиток soft drink

небо sky, heaven

неверный false
негодяй louse (slang)
неделя week
недоставать to be missing (thing)
не за что you're welcome
нездоровый indisposed
некрасивый ugly
немец German
немецкий German (adj.)
немного some, a few, not much, a little
немножко a little
необходимо (dative plus . . .) to have to (мне необходимо I have to)
необходимый necessary
неправильно wrong way
неправный (быть . . .) to be wrong
неприятном положении (быть в . . .) to be in trouble
нерв nerve
несварение indigestion
несколько several, a few
нести to carry
несчастный случай accident
нет no
неудобный uncomfortable
нижняя койка lower berth
низкий low
никакой no, none
никогда never
никто no one, nobody
нитка thread
ничего nothing, it doesn't matter, can't be helped
ничего больше nothing else
ничто none, nothing
но but
новый new
новым (С . . . Годом!) Happy New Year!
нога leg, foot
ноготь nail (finger or toe)
нож knife
нож для бритвы razor blade
ножницы scissors
номер number
норвежец Norwegian
норвежский Norwegian (adj.)
нос nose
носильщик porter
носить to carry, deliver, wear
носки socks
носовой платок handkerchief

ночная жизнь night life
ночная сорочка nightgown
ночной ресторан night club
ночь night
    на . . . overnight
ноябрь November
нравиться to like, please, to be pleasing
    мне нравится I like, it pleases me
нужно need, it is necessary
    мне нужно I need

Оо

о (об, обо) about, concerning
оба both
обед dinner
обедать to dine
обедня Mass
обёрточная бумага wrapping paper
обещать to promise
облако cloud
облачно it is cloudy
облачный cloudy
обокрасть to rob
обход detour
объезд detour
объявить to declare (perf.)
объявлять to declare
объявление declaration
обыкновенный regular, ordinary
обыкновенный орех hazelnut
обыскать to search a person (perf.)
обыскивать to search a person
овощи vegetables
огонь fire
огурец cucumber
одеваться to dress oneself
одежда clothes, clothing
одеколон cologne water
одеться to dress oneself (perf.)
одеяло blanket
один one, alone
одиннадцать eleven
одна, одно one, alone
одном (в . . . направлении) one way
одолжать to lend
одолжить to lend (perf.)
ожерелье necklace

ожог burn
означать to mean, signify (thing as subject)
ой! ouch!
окно window
окно для заказных писем registry window
около about, at, by
оконченный over (finished)
окраска tint
октябрь October
окулист oculist
оливка green olive
омар lobster
он he
она she
они they
оно it
опаздывать to be late, miss a train, etc.
опасность danger, risk
опасный dangerous
опера opera
оповещение notice
опоздать to be late, miss a train, etc.
оптик optician
опять again
оранжад orangeade
орех nut (fruit)
оркестр orchestra
осень autumn, fall
осмотр достопримечательностей sightseeing
оставить to leave behind (perf.)
оставить за to reserve (perf.)
оставить на хранение to check baggage (perf.)
оставлять to leave behind
оставлять за to reserve
оставлять на хранение to check baggage
останавливаться to stop over (train)
остановиться to stop over (train) (perf.)
остановка stay, halt, stop, delay
осторожно! look out!, attention!, careful!
осторожность caution
осторожный careful, cautious
от from (surface)
отбивная котлета chop

отвёртка screwdriver
ответ answer, reply
ответить to answer, reply (perf.)
отвечать to answer, reply
отделить to part, divide, separate (perf.)
отдельно extra, separately
отделять to part, divide, separate
отдохнуть to rest (perf.)
отдых rest, relaxation
отдыхать to rest
отель hotel
отец father
отказаться to refuse (perf.)
отказываться to refuse
открывалка для консервов can opener
открывать to open
открытка post card
открытый open
открыть to open (perf.)
отойти to sail (perf.)
отправитель sender (mail)
отправить to forward (perf.)
отправлять to forward
отход sailing, departure
отходить to sail, leave
отчество patronymic
официант waiter
очень very
очки eyeglasses
очки от солнца sun glasses
ошибка mistake

Пп

падать to fall
пакет package, parcel
палец finger
палуба deck
палубное кресло deck chair
пальто overcoat
памятник monument
пансион boardinghouse
панталоны panties
папироса cigarette

папиросница cigarette case
пара pair
парень guy
парикмахер barber
парикмахерская barbershop
парк park
пароход ship, steamer
паспорт passport
пассажир passenger
пассажирский поезд local train
пастор minister, pastor
педикюр chiropody, foot-care
пелёнка diaper
пепельница ash tray
первая помощь first aid
первый first
перевести to translate (perf.)
перевод money order, bank draft, translation
переводить to translate
переводчик translator
перевязать to bandage (perf.)
перевязывать to bandage
перегреваться to overheat (motor)
перегреться to overheat (motor) (perf.)
перед in front of, before, front part of
переднее освещение headlight
передний front (adj.)
передняя foyer
пережаренный overdone
перекрёсток intersection, crossroad
перелом fracture
перец pepper
перманентная завивка permanent wave
перо pen
перс Persian
персидский Persian (adj.)
персик peach
перцы peppers
перчатка glove
пёс dog
песня song
песок sand
петрушка parsley
петь to sing
печать to seal
печёный baked
печень liver
печь to bake
пешеход pedestrian
пивная saloon, tavern
пиво beer

пиджак jacket, man's coat
пижама pajamas
пикник picnic
пилот pilot
пилюля pill
пипетка dropper
пирог pie
пирожное pastry
писать to write
писчая бумага writing paper
письмо letter
пить to drink
питьё drink, beverage
пищебумажный магазин stationery store
плавать to swim
пластинка phonograph record
пластырь adhesive tape
плата за наём rent
платить to pay
платок shawl
платформа platform
платье dress
плацкартное место reserved seat
плевать воспрещается spitting forbidden
плечо shoulder
плод fruit
пломба filling (tooth)
плоский flat
плоскогубцы pliers
плохо badly, poorly
плохой bad, poor
площадь square (city or town)
плыть to swim
пляж beach
по per
побежать to run (perf.)
поблагодарить to thank (perf.)
побриться to shave oneself (perf.)
поверить to believe, trust (perf.)
повернуть to turn (perf.)
повестка message
повозка horse carriage
поворачивать to turn
поворот turn
повторить to repeat (perf.)
повторять to repeat
повязка bandage
поговорить to speak, talk, say (perf.)
погода weather
погулять to take a walk, walk (perf.)
под under
подарок gift, present

подать to give
подбородок chin
подвязка garter
подержать to keep (perf.), hold a while
поджареный хлеб toast (bread)
подлежит пошлине (it) is dutiable
подливка gravy
подмётка sole (shoe)
поднимать to lift, raise, jack up (car)
поднять to lift, raise, jack up (car) (perf.)
подождать to wait, expect (perf.)
подойти to fit (perf.)
подписать to sign (perf.)
подписывать to sign
подруга friend (fem.)
подтягивать to tighten
подтяжки suspenders
подтянуть to tighten (perf.)
подумать to think (perf.)
подушка pillow
подшипник car bearing
подышать to breathe (perf.)
поезд train
поездка ride, trip
поесть to eat (perf.)
поехать to ride (perf.)
пожаловаться to complain (perf.)
пожалуйста please; you're welcome, don't mention it; help yourself
пожелать to wish, want (perf.)
пожитки belongings
позавтракать to have lunch, breakfast (perf.)
позвать to call, page (perf.)
позволить to allow, permit (perf.)
позвонить to ring (perf.)
поздний late (adj.)
поздно late (adv.)
поздравление congratulations
поиграть to play (perf.)
поймать to catch (perf.)
пойти to go (on foot), walk (perf.)
показать to show (perf.)
показывать to show
поклон greeting, bow
по крайней мере at least
покрахмалить to starch (perf.)
покупать to buy, purchase (perf.)
покупка purchase
покурить to smoke (perf.)
покушать to eat (perf.)

пол floor, sex
пол- half
полдень noon, midday
полезть to climb (perf.)
полёт flight (plane)
полететь to fly (perf.)
полицейская станция police station
полицейский policeman
полиция police
полночь midnight
полный full
полный пансион American plan (room and three meals a day)
половина half (noun)
половой waiter, bellboy, bellhop
положить to put (perf.)
полоскать to rinse (hair, mouth, throat)
полотенце towel
полотно linen
получатель receiver (mail)
получать to receive, get
получать известие to hear from
получать обратно to recover, get back (have given back)
получить to receive, get (perf.)
получить известие to hear from (perf.)
получить обратно to recover, get back (have given back) (perf.)
полюбить to love, like, be fond of (perf.)
польский Polish
поляк Pole
помада pomade
помешанный crazy
помидор tomato
помнить to remember
помогать to help, assist
помочь to help, assist (perf.)
помощь help (noun)
помощник mate (officer)
понадеяться to hope (perf.)
понедельник Monday
понести to carry, deliver, wear (perf.)
понимать to understand
понравиться to please, like, be pleasing (perf.)
понять to understand (perf.)
пообедать to dine (perf.)
пообещать to promise (perf.)
поправить to fix, adjust (perf.)
попрыскать to spray (perf.)

поработать to work (perf.)
порекомендовать to recommend (perf.)
порошок powder
порт port, harbor
портной tailor
портсигар cigarette case
португалец Portuguese (noun)
португальский Portuguese (adj.)
порция portion
порча автомобиля breakdown (car)
порядок order, arrangement
посетить to visit (perf.)
посещать to visit
послать to send (perf.);
    ... по кабелю to cable
послать за to send for (perf.)
после after, afterward
последний last (adj.)
посмеяться to laugh (perf.)
поспешить to hurry, be in a hurry (perf.)
поставить to park (perf.)
постараться to try to (perf.)
постель bed
посторонитесь! gangway!
постричься to get a haircut (perf.)
посылать to send
посылать за to send for
потерять to lose (perf.)
потолок ceiling
потому-что because
потратить to spend (perf.)
потрогать to touch (perf.)
потянуть to pull, draw (perf.)
поцеловать to kiss, embrace (perf.)
поцелуй kiss
почасам by the hour
почему why
починить to repair, mend
починка repairs
почистить to clean, polish, shine (shoes) (perf.);
    ... щёткой to brush
почитать to read (perf.)
почта post office, mail
почти almost, nearly
почтовый ящик letterbox, mailbox
пошлина customs, customs duty
пояс belt
прав right (correct)
правда truth (не правда ли? is it not so?)

правильный true
правый right (opposite of left)
правым (быть ...) to be right
праздник festival
прачешная laundry
прачка laundress
предел скорости speed limit
предельная скорость speed limit
предмет article
предпочесть to prefer (perf.)
предпочитать to prefer
представить to introduce, present (perf.)
представление performance
представлять to introduce, present
прежде before, in the past
прейс курант list (food, wine)
прейс курант вин wine list
прекрасно all right
прибывать to come, arrive
прибыть to come, arrive (perf.)
приветствовать to greet, welcome
привозной imported
приготовить to prepare (perf.)
приготовленный cooked
приготовлять to prepare
приезжать to come, arrive (conveyance)
приехать to come, arrive (conveyance) (perf.)
прийти to come, arrive (on foot) (perf.)
примерить to try on (perf.)
примерять to try on
принадлежать to belong
принести to bring, deliver (perf.)
принимать to accept, receive
приносить to bring, deliver
принять to accept, receive (perf.)
приправленный seasoned
прислужник deck steward
пристань dock, pier
приходить to come, arrive (on foot)
прихожая lobby
причёска set (hair), hair-do
приятный pleasant
прованское масло olive oil
провести время to spend time (perf.)
проводить время to spend time
проводник guide, Pullman porter
проводница hostess, stewardess (plane or train)
програма program

183

продавать to sell
продажа sale
продать to sell (perf.)
продержаться to last (perf.)
продолжать to continue
продолжаться to last
продолжить to continue (perf.)
продолжиться to last (perf.)
проезд fare
проезда (нет . . .) no thoroughfare
прожить to live (perf.)
проколотая шина puncture (tire)
прополоскать to rinse (hair) (perf.)
пропуск pass, permit
просить to ask for, request
проснуться to wake up (perf.)
простите I'm sorry, pardon me
простить to pardon (perf.)
простуда cold (respiratory), chill
простыня bed sheet
просыпаться to wake up
протелеграфировать to telegraph
  (perf.)
протелефонировать to telephone
  (perf.)
протестант Protestant (noun)
протестантский Protestant (adj.)
протечь to leak (perf.)
против against
прохладный cool
проход воспрещается no trespassing
проход запрещён no trespassing
прохода (нет . . .) no thoroughfare
проходить to pass by
прошлый past
прощайте good-by
прощать to pardon
проявить to develop film (perf.)
проявлять to develop film
проясняться to clear up (weather)
проясниться to clear up (weather)
  (perf.)
прямо straight (adv.)
прямой straight (adj.)
птица bird
пуговица button
пудинг pudding
пудра для лица face powder
пустить to let, permit
пустой empty
пустяки! nonsense!
путеводитель guidebook
путевой чек traveler's check

путь way
пьеса play (theater)
пюрэ из mashed
пята heel (of foot)
пятнадцать fifteen
пятница Friday
пятый fifth
пять five
пятьдесят fifty

Pp

раввин rabbi
рагу stew
рад happy, glad
ради Бога! for Heaven's sake!
радиатор radiator
радио radio
радостью (с . . .) gladly, with
  pleasure
раз once
раздражать to annoy, irritate
раздражить to annoy, irritate (perf.)
разменять to cash, change (perf.)
размер measurements, measure
распродажа bargain sale
разрешать to permit, allow, let
разрешить to permit, allow, let
  (perf.)
раковина sink
рана wound
раненый wounded
ранний early (adj.)
рано early (adv.)
раньше earlier
расписание timetable
распухать to swell
распухнуть to swell (perf.)
распухший swollen
ратуша city hall
ребёнок baby, child
ребро rib
редиска radish
регистрационный бланк registra-
  tion blank
резать to cut
резервуар car tank
резина rubber

резиновые каблуки rubber heels
резкий sharp
река river
ремень belt, strap
ремень вентилятора fan belt
рентген X ray
ресница eyelash
рессора mechanical spring
ресторан restaurant
рецепт prescription
рис rice
род kind, sort
родина native country
родители parents
родиться to be born (perf.)
рождаться to be born
Рождество Христово Christmas
розовый pink
роман novel
ростбиф roast beef
рот mouth
рубашка shirt
рука hand
рукав sleeve
руль steering wheel
румын Rumanian
румынский Rumanian (adj.)
румяна rouge
русский Russian (noun and adj.)
ручка двери door handle
ручной работы handmade
ручные часы wrist watch
рыба fish
рынок market
ряд row (theater)

Cc

с with
сад garden
садитесь! all aboard!
садиться to sit down
салад salad
салами salami
сало bacon
салфетка napkin
сам self

самое позднее at the latest
самое худшее worst
самолёт airplane
самопишущее перо fountain pen
самый self, very, most
сандалья sandal
сандвич sandwich
сапог shoe
сардинка sardine
сахар sugar
сварить to cook, boil (perf.)
свежая краска wet paint
свёкла beet
сверх цены cover charge
свесить to weigh (perf.)
свет light, world
светить to shine
световой сигнал stop light
свеча spark plug, candle
свинина pork
свободный free
свой one's own, my own, his own,
    etc. (poss. pron.)
священник priest
сдавать в наём to rent
сдаётся for rent
сдать в наём to rent (perf.)
сделать to do, make (perf.)
север north
сегодня today
сегодня вечером this evening, to-
    night
сегодня ночью tonight
седьмой seventh
сезон season
сейф safe (strongbox)
сейчас right now
семнадцать seventeen
семь seven
семьдесят seventy
семья family
сентябрь September
сердце heart
серебро silver
середина middle
серёжка earring
серый gray
сестра sister
сестра милосердия nurse
сесть to sit down (perf.)
сетка train rack, net
сетка для волос hair net
сигара cigar

185

сиденье seat (in conveyance)
сильный strong
синагога synagogue
синий blue
синяк bruise
сироп syrup
сиять to shine (stars)
сказать to say
скатерть tablecloth
сквозняк draft (current of air)
скидка discount
сколько how much
скоро fast, quickly, soon
сковости gears (car)
скорый fast, quick

скорый поезд express train
скребущий grinding
скрип squeak
слабительное laxative
слабый weak
сладкий sweet
сладкое dessert
сладкое вино sweet wine
следует (как . . .) properly
следующий next
слесарь locksmith
слива plum
сливки cream
слишком много too much
словарь dictionary
слово word
сломанный broken
сломать to break (perf.)
слуга servant, valet
служить to serve
случается happens
случаться to happen
случится will happen
случиться to happen (perf.)
слушать to listen, listen
слушаю! hello! (phone)
слышать to hear
смазать to grease, lubricate (perf.)
смазывать to grease, lubricate
смерть death
смокинг tuxedo
смотреть to look
снаружи outside
снег snow
снимать to take off (clothing)
снимок print (photography)
снова again
снять to take off (clothing) (perf.)

со (see с)
собака dog
собирать to gather, collect
собор cathedral
собрать to gather, collect (perf.)
советский Soviet (adj.)
совсем at all, quite, completely
согласиться to agree (perf.)
соглашаться to agree
сода бикарбоник bicarbonate of soda
Соединённый Штаты Северной Америки U.S.A.
сойти to get off (perf.); . . . с ума to go crazy, lose one's mind
сок juice
солёные огурцы pickles
солёный salty
солнечный sunny
солнце sun
солома straw
соль salt
сонный sleepy
сорок forty
сорочка slip (garment)
сорт sort, kind
состоять из to consist of
соус sauce
Союз Советских Социалистичес-ких Республик U.S.S.R.
спальный вагон sleeping car
спальня bedroom
спаржа asparagus
спасательная одежда life preserver
спасательная лодка life boat
спасибо thanks, thank you
спать to sleep
спеть to sing (perf.)
специальный special
спина back (noun)
спиртной напиток liquor
спичка match
справка information
справочная касса information desk
справочное бюро information bureau
спрашивать to ask, inquire
спросить to ask, inquire (perf.)
спускать to let off (a conveyance)
спускаться to go down
спустить to let off (a conveyance) (perf.)

спуститься to go down (perf.)
спущенная шина flat tire
сразу at once
среда Wednesday
средство remedy
средство от загара sun-tan ointment
средство от насекомых insecticide
С Рождеством Христовым! Merry Christmas!
срочное письмо special delivery
ставить to park
ставня window shutter
стакан drinking glass, tumbler
сталь steel
становиться to become
станция railroad station
стараться to try to
стартер starter
старый old
стать to become (perf.)
стекло glass (material), lens
стена wall
стиль style
сто hundred
стоимость cost, value, worth
стоить to cost, be worth
стой! stop!
стол table
столовая dining room
столовый зал dining salon
стоп! stop!
сторона side
стоянка воспрещается no parking
стоять to stand
стоять в очереди to stand in line
страна country (nation)
страница page
страх fear
страховать to insure
страховка insurance
страховка для путешествующих travel insurance
страшный terrible, awful
стрижка haircut
стручковые бобы string beans
стул chair
стучать to knock
стюардесса stewardess, plane hostess
суббота Saturday
сувенир souvenir
сударь sir

сумашедший crazy
суметь to be able, can, know how (perf.)
сумочка handbag, ladies' pocketbook
сундук trunk
суповая ложка tablespoon(ful)
суповая тарелка soup dish
супруга (ваша . . .) your wife
сутки (в . . .) by the day
сухой dry
сушёная слива prune
сушить to dry
сфотографировать to photograph (perf.)

сходить to get off
сходная цена reasonable price
счастливый happy, lucky
счастье happiness
счёт bill, restaurant check
счётчик taxi meter
считать to count
съездить to drive, travel, go (conveyance) (perf.)
сын son
сыр cheese
сырой damp, rare (meat)
сюда this way

Тт

та that
табак tobacco
табачный магазин cigar store, tobacco shop
табльдот table d'hôte
таблетка tablet
так so
такой such (a)
такси taxi
тальк talcum powder
талья waist
там there
танец dance
танцовать to dance
тарелка plate
тариф hourly rate

твёрдый hard, tough (meat)
те those
театр theater
текучая вода running water
телеграмма telegram
телеграмма по кабелю cable
телеграфировать to telegraph
телеграфировать по кабелю to cable
теленка undershirt
телефон telephone
телефонировать to telephone, phone
телефонистка telephone operator
тело body
телятина veal
тёмный dark
тень shade
  в тени in the shade
теперь now
тёплый warm
термометр thermometer
терять to lose
тётя aunt
течь leak (noun)
течь to leak
тихий quiet
то that
товарищ comrade
товарная почта parcel post
тогда then
тоже also, too
ток высокого напряжения high-tension wires
толкать to push
толкнуть to push (perf.)
толстый thick
только only
только что to have just (with past tense)
томат tomato
тому назад ago
торг bargain
тормоз car brakes
торопить to be in a hurry
тост toast (drink)
тот that (demonstrative)
тот-же same
точка point
тошнит (меня . . .) I am nauseated
трава grass
трамвай trolley, streetcar
тратить to spend (money)
треск rattle (car)
третий third

три three
тридцать thirty
трижды three times
трико panties
тринадцать thirteen
трогать to touch
тротуар sidewalk
трубка smoking pipe
трудный hard (difficult)
туалетная бумага toilet paper
туман fog
туманный foggy
турецкий Turkish
турист tourist
турок Turk
туфли slippers
тысяча thousand
тяжёлый heavy
тянуть to draw, pull

Уу

у at, by
уборная lavatory, washroom, rest room, toilet
увеличение enlargement (photography)
увидеть to see (perf.)
угол corner
угольная бумага carbon paper
удалить to extract (perf.)
удалять to extract
удобный comfortable
удовольствие pleasure
удостоверение certificate, identification
уезжать to leave, depart (conveyance)
уехать to leave, depart (conveyance) (perf.)
ужасный awful, terrible
уже already
ужин supper
узкий narrow
узнать to know (person or fact) (perf.)
укладывать to pack
укол injection

уксус vinegar
улица street
уложить to pack (perf.)
ум mind
у меня кружится голова I feel
   dizzy
универмаг department store
университет university
упасть to drop, fall (perf.)
упереться to lean (perf.)
упираться to lean
употребить to use (perf.)
употребление use
употреблять to use
управляющий manager
уродливый ugly
услышать to hear (perf.)
усталый tired
устрица oyster
утка duck
утра a.m.
утренний чай breakfast
утро morning
утюг flatiron
ухо ear
уходить to leave; depart

Фф

фальшивые зубы denture
фальшивый false
фамилия family name

фар headlight
февраль February
фётр felt
фига fig
фильм movie film, motion picture
фильма film
фойе lounge
фонтан fountain
фотографический аппарат camera
Франция France
француз Frenchman
французский French
фрукт fruit
футбол soccer
фуфайка sweater

Хх

халат dressing gown
химическая чистка dry cleaner's,
   dry cleaning
хинин quinine
хирург surgeon
хлеб bread
хлебосольный hospitable
ходить to walk, go
ходить домой to go home
ходить за покупками to go shopping
холодное мясо cold cuts
холодный cold
хорошенький pretty
хороший good
хорошо good, well
хорошо прожаренный well done
   (steak)
хотеть to want, wish
хотеть пить to be thirsty
хотеть сказать to mean (person as
   subject)
хотеть спать to be sleepy
хотеться to feel like
   мне хочется I feel like
хрусталь crystal
худой bad
худший worst
хуже worse

Цц

цвет color
цветная капуста cauliflower
цветной фильм colored film
цветок flower
целовать to kiss
цена price
цена ночью night rate
центр center

189

цепь chain
церковь church
цыплёнок chicken

что ещё? what else?
что-нибудь anything
что-нибудь ещё? anything else?
что-то something
чувствовать to feel (health)
чулан closet
чулки stockings

чай tea
чайная ложка teaspoon(ful)
час hour
часов (шесть . . .) six o'clock
части spare parts
часто often
часть part
часы watch, clock
чашка cup
чей whose
человек man (human being)
человек! waiter! (when calling to waiter)
челюсть jaw
чемодан valise, suitcase
через through, across, by way of
чернила ink
чёрный black
чёрт devil
чеснок garlic
четверг Thursday
четвёртый fourth
четверть quarter
четыре four
четырнадцать fourteen
чех Czech
чешский Czech (adj.)
чилиец Chilean
чилийский Chilean (adj.)
чинить to mend, repair
число date (calendar)
чистить to clean, shine (shoes)
чистить щёткой to brush
чистый clean
читать to read
чорт devil
чорт возьми! darn it!
что what
что-бы that (conj.)

шаль shawl
шампунь shampoo
шапка cap
шарф scarf
швед Swede
шведский Swedish
швейцар doorman
швейцарец Swiss
швейцарский Swiss (adj.)
шёлк silk
шерсть wool
шестнадцать sixteen
шестой sixth
шесть six
шестьдесят sixty
шея neck
шина tire
шипучее вино sparkling wine
ширина width
широкий wide
шкаф closet, cupboard
школа school
шляпа man's hat
шляпка lady's hat
шнурок shoelace
шоколад chocolate
шоколадные конфеты chocolates
шоссе highway
шофёр driver
шпилька hairpin
шпинат spinach
штаны trousers
штепсель electric switch
штопальная бумага darning cotton
штопать to darn
штопор corkscrew
штора window shade

штраф fine (noun)
шум noise
шумный noisy

Щщ

щека cheek
щётка brush
щётка для одежды clothesbrush
щиколотка ankle

Ээ

экзаменовать to examine
экипаж coach (horse)
эконом purser
экскурсия excursion
экспрес express train
электрическая лампочка flashlight
электрический electric
эликсир lotion
эликсир для волос hair lotion, tonic
эликсир для полосканья рта mouthwash
эта this
эти these
этикетка label
это, этот this

Юю

юбка skirt, petticoat°
ювелир jeweler
ювелирный магазин jewelry shop
юг south
югославянин Yugoslav
югославянский Yugoslavian

Яя

я I
яблоко apple
яд poison
язык tongue, language
яичница omelet
яйцо egg
яйцо в крутую hard-boiled egg
яма hole, dump (slang)
январь January
японец Japanese
японский Japanese (adj.)
ясный clear
ящик drawer, box

Readwell's Widely Read Books

LANGUAGE SERIES

RW-1   Learn English through Hindi

RW-2   Learn Hindi through English

RW-3   Learn Marathi through English

RW-4   Learn Gujarati through English

RW-5   Learn Tamil through English

RW-6   Learn Bengali through English

RW-7   Learn Assamese through English

RW-8   Learn Oriya through English

RW-9   Learn Telugu through English

RW-10   Learn Malayalam through English

RW-11   Learn Urdu through English

RW-12   Learn Kannada through English

RW-13   Learn Punjabi through English

RW-14   Learn French through English/Hindi

RW-15   Learn Arabic through English/Hindi

RW-16   Learn German through English/Hindi

RW-17   Learn Spanish through English

RW-18   Learn Nepali through English

RW-19   Learn Russian through English

RW-20   Learn Italian through English

RW-21   Learn Japanese through English

RW-22   Arabic for Beginners

DICTIONARIES

RW-23   Hindi-English

RW-24   English-Tamil

RW-25   English-Malayalam

RW-26   English-Telugu

RW-27   Marathi-English (Two-colour)

RW-28   English-Hindi (Pocket) (Two-colour)

RW-29   English-Bengali (Pocket) (Two-colour)

RW-30   English-Gujarati (Pocket) (Two-colour)

RW-31   English-English

FORMULAS

• Maths • Physics • Chemistry • Science • Biology

READWELL PUBLICATIONS

B-8, Rattan Jyoti, 18, Rajendra Place
New Delhi-110 008 (INDIA)
Phone : 25737448, 25712649, 5721761; Fax : 91-11-25812385
E-mail : readwell@sify.com
newlight@vsnl.net